The Open University

centre for
**MODERN
LANGUAGES**

A bordo

Get ready for Spanish

ROUTLEDGE

D0257238

L508 project team

Core team

Vivien Bjorck (project secretary)
Dorothy Calderwood (project manager)
Christina Lay (editor)
Cristina Ros i Solé (chair, author and co-ordinator)
Sean Scrivener (editor)
Monica Shelley (academic editor)

Production team

Ann Carter (print buying controller)
Alison Cunningham (project controller)
Jonathan Davies (design group co-ordinator)
Jane Duffield (project controller)
Janis Gilbert (graphic artist)
Siân Lewis (designer)
Jo Parker (liaison librarian)
David Richings (print buying co-ordinator)

BBC production team

Jacqui Charlston (production assistant)
Gerard O'Malley (audio producer)
Dalia Ventura (audio producer)
Penny Vine (audio producer)

Consultant authors

Miguel Giménez López
Raquel de Pedro
Juan Trigo (Audio Drama)

Critical readers

Tita Beaven
Miquel Bonet
Cecilia Garrido
Pat Morton
Hélène Mulphin
Ane Ortega

External assessor

Dr Rob Rix, Trinity and All Saints, Leeds

The project team would like to thank all the people of Toledo who contributed to *A bordo*. Thanks also go to students at Anglia Polytechnic University who tested the materials, to Dr Anne Ife and to Dr Robin Goodfellow.

First published in 1998 by The Open University and Routledge, London.

Copyright © 1998 The Open University

The Open University
Walton Hall, Milton Keynes
MK7 6AA

Edited, designed and typeset by the Open University.

Printed and bound in the United Kingdom by the Alden Group, Oxford.

A catalogue record for this title is available from the British Library.

ISBN 0 415 19899 2

This material may be used as preparation for studying the Open University course *L140 En rumbo: a fresh start in Spanish*. If you would like a copy of *Studying with the Open University* or more information on Open University language materials, please write to the Course Enquiries Data Service, P.O. Box 625, Dane Road, Milton Keynes MK1 1TY, United Kingdom: tel. (00 44) 1908 653231.

Alternatively, much useful course information can be obtained from the Open University's website http://www.open.ac.uk

1.1

L508booki1.1

Índice

¡Bienvenido a bordo!

What is *A bordo*?

This book aims to help you revise your existing skills in Spanish, however you might have acquired them: whether through a formal qualification such as GCSE or 'O' level, or by other routes. You will probably need to spend a minimum of 24 hours studying the book, but this may vary, depending on your level of Spanish.

A bordo means 'On board' and invites you to embark on this short refresher course. A nautical theme has been the inspiration for some of the elements that make up the materials. The term *Atando cabos* is used to signal 'tying up loose ends' in your grammar; *Cabos sueltos* are instances of language usage, such as useful phrases and key expressions; while *Salvavidas* are intended to 'rescue' you by giving you strategies to help you with your learning. These features are represented by the following icons:

Atando cabos

Salvavidas

What is in *A bordo*?

In this pack you will find a book consisting of eight *unidades*, each divided into three *secciones*. Each *sección* is expected to need approximately an hour of study. You will also find three audio cassettes (two C30s and a C60) and a transcript booklet. You will be told when the cassettes relate to the text, but sometimes you may also prefer to listen to them on their own, perhaps while doing something else such as ironing, travelling or simply relaxing. This will work perfectly well, since the pack has been designed for either combined book-and-cassette study or audio work alone.

The Audio Drama Cassette

The Audio Drama (C30) comprises eight episodes of a story set in Madrid and Toledo. The topic covered in each *unidad* is introduced in the first *sección* through the drama. The icon (right) is shown in the margin to remind you to have the cassettes and player ready.

The Activities Cassette

The Activities Cassette (C60) will help you practise your speaking skills. You will participate in dialogues and other interactive exercises. These will normally appear in the second *sección* of each *unidad*.

The Interviews Cassette

A C30 cassette, which contains recordings made on location in Toledo, forms the basis for the third *sección* of each *unidad*. By listening to authentic conversations, you will gain an insight into the lifestyle, interests and traditions of people in this small city in central Spain.

The Transcript Booklet

The Transcript Booklet contains transcripts of the Audio Drama, the Activities Cassette and the Interviews Cassette. It provides a source for several of the *actividades* and can also be used as a resource for further learning.

Promoting learner independence

One of the main aims of this book is to promote independent learning. We have therefore included features to encourage and support you as a learner.

Key learning points are set out at the beginning of each *sección*, and there is a summary of what you should have learned at the end of each *unidad*. Each *unidad* has a short introduction to the theme, to give you a context in which to learn the language. The *unidades* are highly structured in order to guide you better through the learning process. Certain areas of guidance are presented under specific headings:

Atando cabos tells you about the 'nuts and bolts' of Spanish grammar.

Cabos sueltos gives you useful phrases for communicating in particular situations, such as greeting, making suggestions, and so on.

Salvavidas develops your study skills, enabling you to become a more experienced and efficient language learner.

Curiosidades offers unusual facts about Spanish and Spanish American society and culture that have been included specifically with the learner in mind. They echo the topics and themes of the *unidades* and are intended both to give you pleasure and to provide plenty of opportunities to improve your reading skills and extend your vocabulary.

Pronunciación will help you in pronouncing and understanding both Castilian and non-Castilian* forms of Spanish.

Resumen gramatical is for reference, and summarizes all the grammar presented in *A bordo*.

Clave, at the end of the book, provides answers to the *actividades*, together with useful feedback on your mistakes which will help you check on your progress.

* The Spanish spoken in Spanish America, some areas in the north and south of Spain, and in the Canary Isles.

Vocabulary is reinforced at the end of each *unidad* with a variety of *actividades,* such as crosswords or word searches, to provide practice.

Before you begin

In this book you are going to practise communicating in Spanish in everyday situations. You will also learn about Spanish and Spanish-American culture. But before you begin, find out how much you already know. Look at these pictures of places and topics you will encounter in the book and check how many are familiar to you.

Congreso de los Diputados, Madrid

Goya's *La maja vestida*

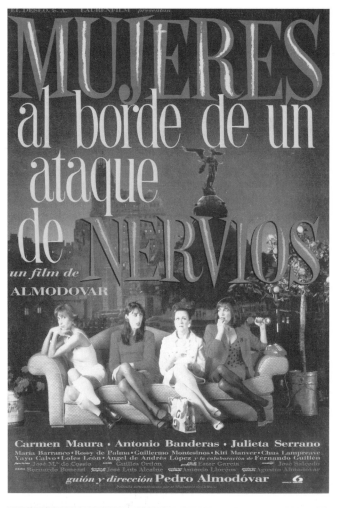

Poster for *Mujeres al borde de un ataque de nervios*

El Patio de la Acequia, jardines del Generalife (Granada)

Poster for *¡Ay, Carméla!*

Un mercadillo en Ciudad de Mexico

Unidad 1 Coincidencias y citas

In *Unidad 1*, you will be working on the Audio Drama *El idioma del amor* and meeting its two main characters, Teresa and Omar, who live in Madrid. You will concentrate on communicating and finding out about Toledo's history and people.

Sección 1

You will listen to the first episode of the Audio Drama, in which the two main characters, Teresa and Omar, meet by chance in a cinema queue in Madrid.

Key learning points

- Greetings and introductions
- Arranging to meet
- Giving and requesting personal information
- Study skills: using the dictionary

Actividad 1.1

Before you listen to the first episode of the Audio Drama, try to remember how you would greet people, depending on what time of the day it is. Match the clocks to the appropriate greeting.

Antes de escuchar la cinta, trate de recordar cómo saludaría a la gente según las diferentes horas del día. Enlace los relojes con el correspondiente saludo.

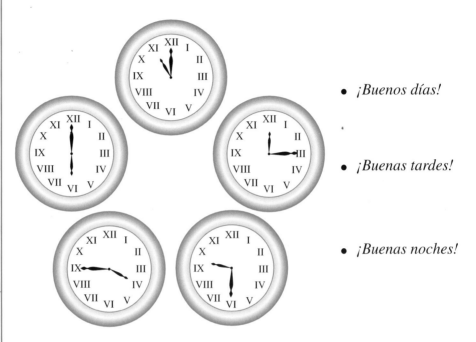

- *¡Buenos días!*

- *¡Buenas tardes!*

- *¡Buenas noches!*

Now read the following information.

Ahora lea la información del recuadro.

Cabos sueltos

Saludos

¡Hola! is a colloquial form which can be used at any time of the day. It often precedes other greetings, for example: *¡Hola! ¡Buenos días!*

¡Buenos días! is used throughout the morning and early part of the afternoon, until lunch-time.

¡Buenas tardes! is used for afternoon (after lunch) and evening.

¡Buenas noches! is used at night-time (not only before going to bed).

Actividad 1.2

Listen to the first episode of the Audio Drama. Don't worry if you can't understand everything: just try to get the gist of what is going on. Make notes while you are listening and answer the questions below.

Escuche el primer episodio del Radiodrama. No se preocupe si no lo entiende todo. Intente comprender lo principal. Tome notas mientras escucha y conteste las preguntas a continuación.

1 Do they address each other formally (*usted*) or informally (*tú*)?

2 Have Omar and Teresa met before?

3 Where are they?

Actividad 1.3

1 Listen to the Audio Drama episode once more and tick which one of the three phrases below Omar uses to introduce himself.

Escuche otra vez la cinta y marque la expresión que usa Omar para presentarse.

(a) Yo me llamo Omar. ❑

(b) Soy Omar Boussidi. ❑

(c) Soy Omar, el nuevo cocinero. ❑

Presentaciones

Me llamo Teresa (Martínez).

Soy Teresa.

Soy Teresa, la nueva profesora.

Responder a presentaciones

Encantado (if you are male).

Encantada (if you are female).

Mucho gusto, which can be used by both males and females.

Hola and *¿Qué tal?*, which are both more informal than the first three expressions.

Presentar a otros

Mira, te presento a Omar. (Informal.)

Le presento al señor Boussidi. (Formal.) Notice the use of the pronoun *le* (in the formal register) to refer to the person to whom you are introducing someone (*les* if you are introducing someone to several people).

In an informal situation, you can just use *éste / ésta* + *es* + the first name:

> *Éste es Omar.*

> *Ésta es Teresa.*

In a more formal setting, you use the title *el señor / la señora / la señorita* before the surname:

> *Ésta es la señora García.*

> *Éste es el señor Pérez.*

2 Now work out the most appropriate phrases according to the formality or informality of the situations given below. Then say them aloud.

Ahora practique en voz alta qué diría en las siguientes situaciones.

(a) You introduce yourself to a friend of a friend.

(b) You introduce Señor Martínez to your new boss.

(c) Your partner introduces you to a member of his family. What would he say?

(d) You have been introduced to a new senior member of staff.

Actividad 1.4

1 Towards the end of their conversation, Teresa and Omar arrange to meet each other the next day. Listen to the last part of the episode once more. Where do they arrange to meet? Answer in Spanish.

Hacia el final, Teresa y Omar quedan para el día siguiente. Vuelva a escuchar la cinta. ¿Dónde quedan?

2 Listen once more and write down the expressions Teresa and Omar use to arrange to meet.

Escuche otra vez el extracto y anote las expresiones que usan Teresa y Omar para quedar.

¿Cómo quedamos?

Here are some expressions that you can use when making arrangements to meet:

¿A qué hora quedamos? is used to arrange a time.

¿Cómo quedamos? is used to make more general arrangements (time, place and so on).

¿Le parece bien…? is a formal way of asking 'Is it OK if…?'

¿Te parece bien…? is an informal way of asking 'Is it OK if…?'

Muy bien is the usual way of showing agreement.

Vale is an informal expression of agreement, like 'Fine'.

3 Listen to the last part of the episode once more, concentrating on the expressions used to say good-bye. Which ones did Omar and Teresa use? Write them down.

Ahora anote las expresiones que usan para despedirse.

Despedidas

Spanish has several expressions for saying good-bye:

¡Adiós! means 'Good-bye!' and it often precedes other farewell expressions, for example:

> *¡Adiós! ¡Hasta luego!*

¡Hasta luego! means 'See you later!' and it is used even when you have made no arrangement to see each other again.

¡Hasta mañana! means 'See you tomorrow!'

Using the dictionary

Your dictionary will be one of your most useful tools while you are learning a language. When you look up a word in the dictionary, try to get more information than just the translation. Most dictionaries describe the type of word it is (adjective, noun, verb and so on) and, where appropriate, give its gender. The bilingual dictionary will give an example, the translation and, sometimes, different meanings for the word.

Look at the following dictionary entry for *cocina, cocinar* and *cocinero* and take note of the different kinds of information mentioned.

cocina *f* **-1.** [habitación] kitchen. **-2.** [electrodoméstico] cooker, stove; ~ **eléctrica/de gas** electric/gas cooker. **-3.** [arte] cooking; ~ **española** Spanish cuisine ○ cooking; **libro/clase de** ~ cookery book/class.
cocinar *vt & vi* to cook.
cocinero, -ra *m y f* cook.

(Larousse Pocket Spanish Dictionary, 1994)

Actividad 1.5

1 Before you listen to the first episode again, read the words in the box below. They all occur on the cassette, but only four of them are the names of jobs. Which four? Use the dictionary if there are some words you do not know.

Antes de escuchar el episodio otra vez, lea las palabras en el recuadro. Todas aparecen en la grabación, pero sólo cuatro son nombres de profesiones. Intente identificarlas. Use el diccionario si no comprende alguna de las palabras.

> domingo, actor, extranjero, estudiar, ingeniero, profesor, monedero, cocinero, película, puerta

2 Now write down the four words that describe people by their professions and, with the help of your dictionary, try to find the equivalents for the opposite sex.

Ahora escriba esas cuatro palabras y, con la ayuda del diccionario, intente encontrar sus equivalentes para el género opuesto.

Masculino	Femenino

Atando cabos

Género y número

Nouns are either masculine (*el coche*) or feminine (*la mesa*), but those that can refer to both men and women, such as their professional roles, can be either masculine or feminine.

The difference between the masculine and feminine forms of nouns can be indicated in various ways:

1   You can add an *a* to the masculine form. This is what happens when the latter ends in a consonant, as in:

> *pintor / pintora*
>
> *conductor / conductora*
>
> *escritor / escritora*

2   You can replace the final *o* of the masculine form with an *a*:

> *camarero / camarera*
>
> *peluquero / peluquera*
>
> *abogado / abogada*

3   There are also some irregular pairs, such as:

> *actor / actriz*

4   Certain nouns do not change. They can be used as either masculine or feminine forms. Examples are:

> *el/la modelo*
>
> *el/la deportista*

Cabos sueltos

¿De qué trabaja?

When you indicate your profession, the article (that is *el, la, un, una*) is not used. So you would say:

> *Soy médico.*   I am a doctor.

You would also use the verb *ser* to say what someone is qualified to do:

> *Omar es ingeniero.*

The expression *trabajar de* indicates the work someone does:

> *Omar trabaja de cocinero.*

Other expressions that you may find useful include:

tener una tienda	to have / own a shop
ser el propietario / la propietaria de un negocio	to be the owner of a [small] business
estar en el paro	to be unemployed
estar jubilado, -a	to be retired

Actividad 1.6

1 At the beginning of the first episode of the Audio Drama, the narrator gives you some personal details about Teresa. What sort of thing do you expect to be mentioned? Tick the information you think you will hear and then do step 2 before checking the *Clave*.

En la segunda parte del episodio, el narrador nos da unos detalles personales de Teresa. Marque la información que espera escuchar.

(a) How old she is. ❑

(b) Where she lives. ❑

(c) Where she comes from. ❑

(d) What her hobbies are. ❑

(e) Whether she is married. ❑

(f) How many brothers and sisters she has. ❑

(g) What her mother's name is. ❑

2 Now listen to the cassette and check whether you were right or not.

Ahora escuche la cinta y compruebe si tenía razón o no.

3 Read the following descriptions of Teresa and Omar, then listen to the episode again. You will find that the information below is not accurate. Correct it according to what you hear on the cassette.

Escuche de nuevo el episodio y corrija la información a continuación.

Teresa tiene treinta años. No tiene hijos. Vive en Toledo. Trabaja en la universidad. Es profesora de alemán. Su madre, doña Amelia, vive en Madrid con su marido.

Omar tiene veinte años. Es bastante bajo. Vive en Madrid, pero es de Argelia. Trabaja de ingeniero. Quiere aprender inglés. Su madre también vive en Madrid, pero es francesa.

Actividad 1.7

1 Now write a similar description of yourself. You will have to change the form of the verbs. First, can you remember which forms you need to use for 'I'?

Ahora escriba un párrafo similar sobre sí mismo / misma. Tendrá que cambiar las formas verbales. Averigüe primero cuáles tiene que usar para la forma 'yo'.

Infinitivo	el/ella/Ud.	yo
llamarse	se llama	**ejemplo**: Me llamo Julia
tener	tiene	
vivir	vive	
trabajar	trabaja	
ser	es	
querer	quiere	

2 Memorize what you have just written and say it aloud without looking at the table. This will help fix these new forms in your memory and give you confidence in using them.

Memorice lo que acaba de escribir y, sin mirar el texto, practíquelo en voz alta.

In more formal contexts, for example when completing job or passport application forms, you will be asked for personal information in quite a different way from an informal request.

Actividad 1.8

1 Read Omar and Teresa's identity cards and try to understand what the words mean. You will notice that several lines have been left incomplete in our version.

Lea el contenido de los carnets de identidad e intente entender lo que significan las palabras.

CARNET DE IDENTIDAD N. 0055903

Apellidos: Martínez
Nombre: Teresa
Nacionalidad:
Profesión:
Estado civil:
Lugar de nacimiento: Toledo
Domicilio: c/ Cava Alta, 23. Madrid.

CARNET DE IDENTIDAD N. 0075452

Apellidos: Boussidi
Nombre: Omar
Nacionalidad: *Marroci*
Profesión: *Cocinero*
Estado civil: *ingeniero*
Lugar de nacimiento: Casablanca, Marruecos.
Domicilio: c/ Marqués de Santa Ana, 2. Madrid.

2 Listen to the first episode again and fill in the missing information. If there is something you still don't understand, read the transcript while you listen to the cassette once more.

Escuche el primer episodio otra vez y complete la ficha con la información que falta.

3 Below is a visa application form for a trip to Spain. Complete it with your personal details.

Complete el siguiente visado de España con su información personal.

ESPAÑA MINISTERIO DE ASUNTOS EXTERIORES	SOLICITUD DE VISADO: ....
MISIÓN DIPLOMÁTICA U OFICINA CONSULAR:	
1. APELLIDOS .... 2. OTROS APELLIDOS .... 3. NOMBRES .... 4. SEXO .... 5. LUGAR Y FECHA DE NACIMIENTO .... 6. PAÍS .... 7. NACIONALIDAD/ES ACTUAL/ES .... 8. ESTADO CIVIL	FOTOGRAFÍA RECIENTE

(Arnal, Carmen and Ruiz de Garibay, Araceli, «Escribe en español», *Español por destrezas,* Sociedad General Española de Librería (SGEL), 1996, p. 11)

¿ESTADO CIVIL, ABUELA?

~/PÚUUH!....TODOS, M'HIJITO.

Estados civiles

(Quino, *El País Semanal,* 29 de diciembre 1996)

Sección 2

One way to practise your language skills in Spain or Spanish America is to set up a conversation exchange. In *Sección 2*, you start by looking at items on a noticeboard, where you can choose a suitable person to practise with. When you arrive in a new place, you'll also need some basic telephone skills, which you will also develop in this *sección*.

> **Key learning points**
> - Giving and understanding physical descriptions
> - Spelling words
> - Talking on the phone
> - Study skills: checking you've understood

Actividad 1.9

1   In the *Escuela Oficial de Idiomas*, where Teresa works, there is a noticeboard for people to display advertisements about accommodation, conversation practice and items wanted. Read the following three advertisements put up by people looking for conversation practice. Which offer would you choose?

Fíjese en los anuncios de diferentes personas buscando a alguien para hacer intercambio de conversación en lengua extranjera. ¿Cuál escogería?

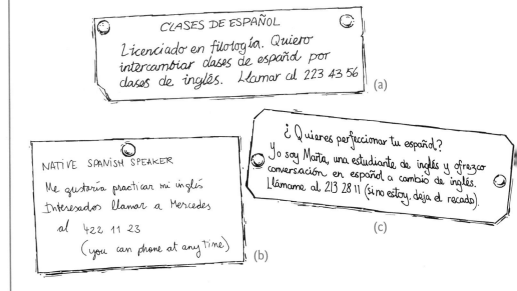

CLASES DE ESPAÑOL

Licenciado en filología. Quiero intercambiar clases de español por clases de inglés. Llamar al 223 43 56

(a)

NATIVE SPANISH SPEAKER

Me gustaría practicar mi inglés Interesados llamar a Mercedes al 422 11 23

(you can phone at any time)

(b)

¿Quieres perfeccionar tu español? Yo soy Marta, una estudiante de inglés y ofrezco conversación en español a cambio de inglés. Llámame al 213 28 11 (si no estoy, deja el recado).

(c)

2 Below are drawings of three people. The first one is described for you. Now you describe the other two. If you want to revise how to describe people, read *Atando cabos* first and then go back to this activity.

Describa a las otras dos personas de los dibujos.

Jesús tiene unos cuarenta años. Tiene barba y es alto. Lleva pantalones y camisa.

María ●●●●●●●●●●●

Rosa ●●●●●●●●●●●

Atando cabos

Descripción de personas

There are three verbs that are commonly used when talking about what people look like:

ser (ser alto); *llevar* (llevar vaqueros); *tener* (tener bigote).

They can be used with various adjectives or nouns:

ser		llevar		tener	
	bajo		unos pantalones		cuarenta años
	flaco		una camisa		barba
	rubio		gafas		pecas
	moreno		barba		el pelo rubio
	alto				
	mayor				
	joven				

For example:

Soy flaco, llevo una camisa azul y tengo cuarenta años.

3 Now write a description of yourself.

Ahora haga una descripción de sí mismo / misma.

You are going to meet your chosen person for conversation practice. You need to phone him or her and make arrangements to meet somewhere. To be able to recognize each other, you must each give a physical description of yourself.

Something else you might need to do when you phone this person is to spell your name, and perhaps the street or tube stop where you are going to meet.

Actividad 1.10

1 Listen to the alphabet in Extract 1 (part one) of the Activities Cassette. Listen to the way the letters are pronounced. Repeat each one till you are confident you know it.

Escuche el abecedario y repita cada letra hasta que esté seguro de saber pronunciarlo.

   a, be, ce, de, e, efe, ge, hache, i, jota, ka, ele, elle, eme, ene, eñe, o, pe, cu, erre, ese, te, u, uve, uve doble, equis, i griega, zeta.

2 Listen to the spelling of some Spanish surnames given in the Activities Cassette, Extract 1 (part two) and repeat their pronunciation.

Escuche cómo se deletrean los nombres de la cinta.

3 Listen again to the Spanish names in the same extract and write them down.

Escuche los nombres otra vez y escríbalos.

Actividad 1.11

1 Listen to the conversation in Extract 2 (part one). A Spaniard is phoning an English-speaking person to do a language exchange. What is the British person called? Listen to the extract as many times as you want. Rewind and pause as necessary.

Escuche la conversación sobre un estudiante que quiere hacer un intercambio de español–inglés. ¿Cómo se llama la persona británica?

2 Now go to Extract 2 (part two) and practise the same dialogue by playing the part of the Briton in the gapped recording. If you find it too difficult, try reading the transcript first and, once you are more familiar with the dialogue, try again with the cassette.

Ahora practique el diálogo, haciendo el papel de la persona británica.

3 Listen to the continuation of the telephone conversation in Extract 2 (part three), and answer the following questions.

Escuche la continuación de la conversación telefónica y conteste las siguientes preguntas.

(a) ¿Cómo se llama la persona española?

(b) ¿Dónde quedan?

Checking you've understood

When you are in a conversation with somebody you might fail to hear or understand enough to follow what they are saying. This might be because of background noise, because you have never heard some word or phrase before, or simply because they were talking too fast for you to take it in. Such breakdowns of communication are quite usual, especially in the early stages of learning a language.

Learning a few phrases to tackle such problems will help you. There are some in the dialogue above:

¿Cómo se escribe?   *(How do you spell it?)*

¿Puede repetirlo, por favor?   *(Can you repeat that, please?)*

¿Cómo dice?   *(What did you say?)*

You might just repeat part of the sentence leading up to the bit that has not been heard, for example: *¿ Vive en...?* ('You live in...?').

4   Listen to Extract 2 (part four) and practise the same dialogue by playing the part of the Briton in the gapped recording.

Escuche y practique el diálogo haciendo el papel de la persona británica.

When you arrive somewhere new, you often need to track down useful phone numbers.

Actividad 1.12

1   Go to Extract 3 of the Activities Cassette and ask the operator for some useful phone numbers.

Pregunte al servicio de información algunos teléfonos útiles.

Números de teléfono

¿Me podría decir el número de...?   (Could you tell me the number for...?)

In Spanish, phone numbers are usually given in pairs: so the number 2546578 would be given as 2 / 54 / 65 / 78, leaving the first number on its own. Alternatively, you could say each number separately.

When you answer the phone you usually say *¿Diga?* or *¿Dígame?*

2 Now practise saying a few phone numbers in Spanish. Write down the following numbers as specified and then read the sentences aloud. If you don't know how to say two-digit numbers, then say them separately.

Ahora practique cómo decir números de teléfono en español. Escriba los números de teléfono que se le piden y lea las frases en voz alta.

Mi teléfono particular es el ......

El teléfono de mi trabajo es el ......

El prefijo internacional desde mi país es el ......

El número de información telefónica es el ......

Spanish is spoken not only in Spain and Spanish America, but also in parts of Africa and Asia. It is the second most widely spoken language in the world and, despite the differences in pronunciation, grammar and vocabulary, nearly 400 million native speakers understand each other without major difficulties.

Actividad 1.13

1 There are many parts of the world where Spanish is exclusively or widely spoken. How many of the countries / areas can you name?

El español se habla en muchas partes del mundo. ¿Cuántas puede nombrar?

1	8	15	22 ....
2	9	16	23 ....
3	10	17	24 ....
4	11	18	25 ....
5	12	19	26 ....
6	13	20	27 ....
7	14	21	28 ....

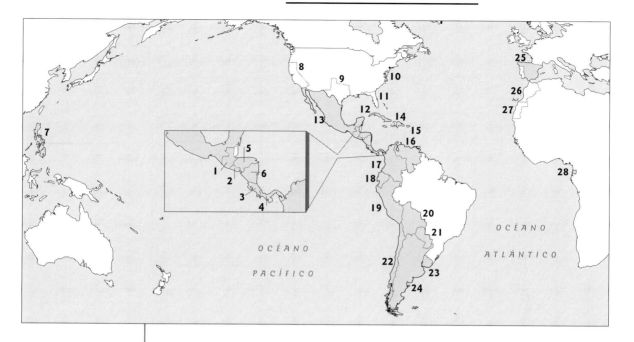

2 Some names of other countries, nationalities and languages are given below. Although the words for the nationality and the language are quite often the same, there are many cases where this is not true. Fill the gaps in this table with the appropriate forms.

Rellene los espacios del siguiente cuadro con las formas apropiadas en relación a países, nacionalidades e idiomas.

¡Ojo! Remember that in Spanish, unlike English, adjectives referring to nationality and language do **not** have capital letters at the beginning.

Soy de... Inglaterra	Soy... inglés / inglesa	Hablo... inglés
Rusia	ruso / rusa	ruso
	francés / francesa	
		italiano
Suecia		
	alemán / alemana	
	estadounidense	
Marruecos		

Sección 3

In this *sección*, you will learn about Toledo, a small city near Madrid which was once the capital of the kingdom of Castile and is now the seat of the autonomous government of Castilla–La Mancha.

Key learning points

- Describing places
- Agreement of adjectives and nouns
- Basic pronunciation: the vowel sounds
- Study skills: listening for gist

Actividad 1.14

Plaza de Zocodover, Toledo

1   This is what two famous Spanish writers have said about Toledo:

> *Toledo fue una ciudad oriental avanzada en el Oeste.*
>
> (Gregorio Marañón)
>
> *Toledo es una historia de España completa.*
>
> (Benito Pérez Galdós)

What do these quotations suggest to you about Toledo?

Curiosidad~

está en el corazón
it's in the heart, in the
centre

Toledo está en el corazón mismo de la península ibérica. Es una ciudad histórica y monumental que sintetiza tres importantes culturas que han pasado por España: la cristiana, la judía y la musulmana. Esta riqueza de pasado cultural se refleja en la arquitectura del lugar. En Toledo también hay varios museos para visitar. Otro atractivo de esta ciudad es la Plaza de Zocodover, la antigua plaza del mercado árabe donde todavía tienen lugar mercados de artesanía. Actualmente, a pesar de estar tan lejos de los centros turísticos de la costa, es una de las ciudades más visitadas en España por su atractivo cultural.

artesanía
arts and crafts or
handicrafts

2 Tick the adjectives you would choose to describe Toledo.

Marque los adjetivos que escogería para describir Toledo.

industrial	☐	exótica	☐	antigua	☑
pequeña	☑	provinciana	☐	costera	☐
despoblada	☐	histórica	☑	famosa	☑
artística	☑	desconocida	☐	turística	☑

Actividad 1.15

Before you listen to a description of Toledo, read these three short descriptions of different Spanish-speaking cities. Match each city with its correct description.

Lea las tres descripciones de ciudades y decida a qué ciudad se refieren.

(a) Granada

(b) Cuzco

(c) Madrid

(i) Está justo en el centro del país, es la capital y tiene un gran parque en el centro cerca de un museo de pintura muy famoso.

(ii) Es una ciudad muy bonita en el sur de España. Tiene un palacio de origen árabe muy conocido y un barrio de casas blancas muy famoso, llamado el Albaicín.

(iii) Es muy antigua y está en las montañas, a gran altitud. Era la capital del antiguo imperio inca. Conserva numerosas ruinas de esa época.

Among Toledo's attractions are its beautiful streets and buildings, as you will hear in the next *actividad*.

Actividad 1.16

1 In Extract 1 of the Interviews Cassette, two people are describing Toledo. Listen to what they say and then write a sentence in Spanish to describe what the city is like. Before you listen, read the advice overleaf.

En la Cinta de entrevistas, va a escuchar a dos personas hablando de Toledo. Escriba en una frase cómo es la ciudad de Toledo.

Listening for gist

In this *actividad* you will listen to an authentic recording of a Spanish person speaking at normal speed. Don't worry if you don't understand it at first. Try to listen for the general meaning, using as many clues as you can from the context: you already know that these people are from Toledo; what they are going to talk about, i.e. their city; and you already know something about Toledo. You can also pick up key words to guide you through the meaning of the passage.

2   Listen to Extract 1 again and tick the adjectives that you hear from the following list.

Escuche el Extracto 1 y marque cuáles de los siguientes adjetivos aparecen en la grabación.

medieval	☑	grande	❑	importante	❑
antiguo	☑	famoso	☑	bonito	☑
nuevo	❑	turístico	❑	pequeño	☑

Atando cabos

Concordancia de adjetivos y nombres

In Spanish, adjectives (*antiguo, artístico*, for example) agree in gender and number with the nouns they describe:

> una cas**a** antigu**a**
>
> unos monument**os** artístic**os**

Concordancia de género

You saw earlier that nouns frequently end in *o* (*el chico*) when masculine and *a* (*la chica*) when feminine. However, if the noun ends in a consonant (*la ciudad*) or in *e* (*el hombre*) you will only be able to know the gender from the article (*el, la, un, una*).

Look at the examples below:

> **el** *árbol viejo* (masc.)
>
> **el** *restaurante italiano* (masc.)
>
> **la** *cantante americana* (fem.)
>
> **la** *estación ferroviaria* (fem.)
>
> **un** *camión extranjero* (masc.)
>
> **una** *catedral gótica* (fem.)

Concordancia de número

As a general rule, the plural of nouns and adjectives is formed by adding *s* when the word ends in a vowel (*restaurante* + *s* = *restaurantes; grande* + *s,* = *grandes*); or *es*, when it ends in a consonant (*ciudad* + *es* = *ciudades; azul* + *es* = *azules*).

Here are some more examples:

> *los edificios grandes*
>
> *las iglesias románicas*
>
> *unos bancos abiertos*
>
> *unas pensiones baratas*

3 Here is an incomplete transcript of what you have just heard. Fill in the gaps by writing down the missing adjectives. Remember that the adjective needs to agree with the noun it describes. Check what you have done by listening to the extract again.

Complete la transcripción del extracto con los adjetivos apropiados del siguiente recuadro.

> pequeño, bonito, artístico, diverso, importante, amurallado, gótico, significativo, medieval, famoso

— ¿Cómo es Toledo?

— Es muy *bonita* porque es una ciudad antigua. Es *medieval* y tiene calles *pequeñas* y edificios muy bonitos, antiguos.

— ¿Por qué es tan *famosa* Toledo?

— ¿Toledo? Famosa por supuesto, por su historia, por su arte. Toda ella es historia y es arte.

— Es famosa, además por sus monumentos *artísticos*, porque han pasado muchas culturas por aquí. Ha habido árabes, judíos, cristianos… y es un centro de unión de gentes de pueblos *diversos*.

— ¿Qué hay para visitar?

— Está la catedral de Toledo, que es muy bonita, del siglo *XIII*, ¿eh? Luego tienes por ejemplo también el Alcázar, San Juan de los Reyes, que es un monasterio. Hay palacios donde vivieron nobles *importantes* de la antigüedad.

Now read about another very famous city, Mexico City.

4 Practise agreeing adjectives and nouns by filling in the gaps in this description of Mexico City.

Practique la concordancia de los adjetivos, rellenando los huecos en la descripción de la ciudad de México.

La ciudad de México, uno de los mayores focos cultural_ de América Latina, es hoy una gran urbe modern_ que concentra más de 20 millones de habitantes. En sus calles se entremezclan pasado, presente y futuro. La plaza del Zócalo, la más grande y antigu_ de la ciudad, el Castillo de Chapultepec, el maravillos_ Museo Arqueológico, obra maestra de culturas milenarias, la Zona Ros_, área peatonal y donde se encuentran unos comercios muy lujos_, o el bonit_ barrio de Coyoacán donde vivió la famos_ pintora Frida Kahlo y su esposo, el conocid_ muralista Diego Rivera.

Actividad 1.17

1 Imagine you are in Toledo and have just met a local person and you want to ask him/her lots of questions. Read these jumbled-up questions about Toledo and put them in the order in which you would ask them.

Lea las siguientes preguntas sobre Toledo y ordénelas.

¿Cómo es la gente en Toledo?   11

¿Cómo te llamas?   **1**

¿Cuánto tiempo hace que vives aquí?   4

¿Qué idiomas hablas?   10

¿Eres de aquí?   2

Y tu familia, ¿de dónde es?   3

¿Por qué es tan famosa Toledo?   6

¿Hay muchos turistas en Toledo?   8

¿Cómo es Toledo?   5

¿Qué hay para visitar?   7

¿De qué países son los turistas?   9

2 Listen to Extract 2 of the Interviews Cassette to check the order in which the questions are asked.

Escuche el Extracto 2 para comprobar en qué orden se han hecho las preguntas.

Actividad 1.18

Go to Extract 4 of the Activities Cassette, where you are asked to provide personal information. Check the *Clave* for a model answer.

Dé sus datos personales.

Pronunciación y ortografía

Spanish has very straightforward pronunciation: its sounds are pronounced as they are written. One of the most distinctive features of Spanish is the clarity of its vowel sounds, of which it has only five. These correspond to the five vowels *a*, *e*, *i*, *o* and *u*. They are always pronounced in the same way, whether they are stressed or unstressed, unlike in English.

Actividad 1.19

1   Listen to this traditional Spanish children's rhyme in Extract 5 (part one) of the Activities Cassette, and note how the vowels are pronounced. Don't look at the text for the moment.

Escuche la siguiente rima infantil y fíjese en cómo se pronuncian las vocales.

2   Listen again, this time looking at the text.

Escuche otra vez mirando el texto.

A la lata, al latero

A la lata, al latero
A la chica del chocolatero.
A la 'a', a la 'a',
Mariquita no sabe planchar.
A la 'e', a la 'e',
Mariquita no sabe barrer.
A la 'i', a la 'i',
Mariquita no sabe escribir.
A la 'o', a la 'o',
Mariquita no sabe el reloj.
A la 'u', a la 'u',
¡Mariquita eres tú!

3   This time, listen to the rhyme on the Activities Cassette Extract 5 (part two) and repeat each verse.

Esta vez, escuche la rima y repita cada verso.

Actividad 1.20

Descripción escondida

Hidden in this box are 11 words relating to physical descriptions: *vestido, gordo, pecas, rubio, bajo, alto, gafas, años, bigote, barba* and *ojos*. They may be found in any direction: upwards, downwards, from right to left or from left to right.

Busque las 11 palabras escondidas en este cuadro. Están dispuestas en cualquier sentido o dirección.

e	b	u	s	e	y	l	a	i	r
b	a	t	a	h	t	u	k	c	a
c	r	o	ñ	u	c	o	f	e	b
s	o	j	o	n	a	e	g	o	r
a	v	e	s	t	i	d	o	i	a
b	e	r	o	i	b	u	r	t	b
e	u	j	n	a	s	a	d	i	i
g	a	r	t	a	l	t	o	d	l
b	i	o	f	s	e	a	r	i	t
n	s	a	c	e	p	i	t	o	f
u	g	a	l	e	b	u	r	a	k

Resumiendo...

Now you can:

- greet and introduce people
- arrange to meet
- ask for and give personal information
- ask for and give descriptions of people and places
- make nouns and adjectives agree
- spell words
- have a simple conversation on the phone

Unidad 2 *Buenas noticias*

In the next episode of the Audio Drama, Omar and Teresa go to the *Escuela Oficial de Idiomas*, where Omar enrols for a course in Spanish cultural studies. The second *sección* focuses on means of communication old and new – letter, telephone and the Internet – and their advantages and disadvantages. In the last *sección* you will listen to an interview with two postal workers in Toledo who give their views on the changing nature of their job.

Sección 1

In the second episode of *El idioma del amor*, Omar discovers that a wide variety of languages are spoken in Spain. Even though Castilian (usually referred to as Spanish) is the official language of the whole country, there are three other official languages: Catalan, Galician and Basque (also known as Euskera).

Key learning points

- Talking about the recent past
- Describing moods and character
- Study skills: writing business letters

Actividad 2.1

The five people in the photographs below are from different areas of Spain. Read the captions about where they come from and link them to the correct areas on the map.

Las personas de los dibujos son de diferentes zonas de España. Lea los pies de foto y únalos con las áreas correspondientes en el mapa.

Las autonomías de España

Me llamo Antonio Martínez. Soy de Soria, pero ahora vivo en Francia y no hablo mi lengua, el castellano, con mucha frecuencia.

Soy Begoña Iturriate. Nací en Bilbao, que está en la costa norte de España. En casa siempre hablo vasco.

Me llamo Montse Fuente. Soy del noreste de la península. Con mis amigos hablo catalán, pero con mis padres hablo en castellano.

Me llamo Moncho Pardo. Soy de una región en el noroeste de España. Hablo dos lenguas españolas: castellano y gallego.

¡Hola! Soy Ana Almeida. Nací en el sur, en Sevilla. Aunque vivo en Madrid, no he perdido mi acento andaluz.

Actividad 2.2

Listen to the second episode of the Audio Drama, *Las clases de cultura española,* and choose the eight verbs from the list below that describe what Teresa and Omar have just been doing.

Ahora escuche el segundo episodio del Radiodrama y escoja los ocho verbos que indican lo que Teresa y Omar acaban de hacer.

saludar ❑	preguntar ❑	correr ❑
ir (a algún sitio) ❑	explicar ❑	invitar ❑
cantar ❑	comer ❑	quedar ❑
tomar (algo) ❑	pasear ❑	decir (adiós) ❑

Atando cabos

Pretérito perfecto

To talk about what people **have done** in Spanish, the perfect tense (*pretérito perfecto*) is used. The table below shows how it is formed.

	auxiliary	-ar	-er	-ir
(yo)	he	cantado	comido	vivido
(tú)	has	cantado	comido	vivido
(él, ella, Ud.)	ha	cantado	comido	vivido
(nosotros, -as)	hemos	cantado	comido	vivido
(vosotros, -as)	habéis	cantado	comido	vivido
(ellos, ellas, Uds.)	han	cantado	comido	vivido

As you can see, the perfect tense is formed by using the present tense of the auxiliary verb *haber* (*he, has, ha, hemos, habéis, han*) followed by the past participle of the main verb (*cantado, comido, vivido*).

The past participle is formed as follows:

- verbs whose infinitives end in -*ar* take –**ado** as an ending.

- verbs whose infinitives end in -*er* or -*ir* take –**ido** as an ending.

In certain irregular verbs the past participle does not conform to the rule above. A few of them are given below:

decir	→	*dicho*	*poner* → *puesto*	
hacer	→	*hecho*	*romper* → *roto*	
morir	→	*muerto*	*volver* → *vuelto*	

The perfect tense is mainly used to talk about an event that has taken place within a period of time that is still continuing:

Hoy no he visto las noticias en la tele.	I haven't seen the news on TV today.
Este mes he recibido muchas cartas.	I have received lots of letters this month.
Esta semana he ido al cine dos veces.	This week I've been to the cinema twice.
Esta mañana no he oído al cartero.	I didn't hear the postman this morning.*

*Notice that the use of the perfect tense in English does not correspond exactly to the use of the *pretérito perfecto* in Spanish.

Non-Castilian speakers tend to use the preterite (*fui, escribí, estudié, volví*) when talking about recent events.

Actividad 2.3

Carmen has come to see her mother, Teresa, who chats about what she has been doing. The sketches below represent her memories, with an appropriate verb for each. Think about the order in which the events probably occurred. Then, using the perfect tense, write down what Teresa might say about them.

Teresa le explica a Carmen lo que ha hecho hoy. Mire los dibujos y escriba frases usando los verbos en el pretérito perfecto.

Ejemplo

recoger   He recogido a Omar.

dar

charlar

ir

tomar

Actividad 2.4

Listen to the second episode of the Audio Drama again. Then decide whether the statements below are true or false and tick the correct boxes. You may need to listen to the whole episode or certain passages several times.

Escuche otra vez el Radiodrama e indique si las siguientes frases son verdaderas o falsas. Puede escuchar el episodio o partes de él varias veces.

		Verdadero	Falso
1	Teresa ha sido puntual.	☐	☑
2	Omar está enfadado.	☐	☑
3	Omar es agresivo con la persona encargada de las matrículas.	☐	☑
4	Omar tiene curiosidad por el curso.	☑	☐
5	Teresa no está bien informada sobre las lenguas de España.	☐	☑
6	Omar está interesado en la explicación de Teresa.	☑	☐
7	España es muy variada lingüísticamente.	☑	☐
8	Teresa quiere irse porque está aburrida.	☐	☑
9	Teresa está contenta porque Omar la invita al cine.	☑	☐
10	Omar ha sido muy amable con Teresa.	☑	☐

Atando Cabos

Describir con 'ser' y 'estar'

You will have noticed that both *ser* and *estar* can be used in descriptions of moods or characteristics.

Usually, *ser* is followed by words that denote characteristic features, for example:

- *ser alegre*   *Es un chico muy alegre.*
- *ser divertido, -a*   *Es un libro muy divertido.*
- *ser agresivo, -a*   *Es una chica un poco agresiva.*

Estar is used when followed by words that describe mood, for example:

- *estar enfadado, -a* *Hoy Teresa está enfadada.*
- *estar contento, -a* *Los dos están muy contentos.*
- *estar triste*   *Hoy está un poco triste.*

Actividad 2.5

Look back at the statements in *Actividad 2.4* about the Audio Drama and make two lists: one using phrases where *ser* is more appropriate, the other where *estar* is more correct.

Ahora mire las frases del Radiodrama y haga dos listas, una con ejemplos del verbo 'estar' y otra con ejemplos del verbo 'ser'.

Curiosidad~

títulos
qualifications

Las Escuelas Oficiales de Idiomas son centros públicos dependientes del Ministerio de Educación y Cultura español donde se dan clases de lenguas. Sus títulos son reconocidos oficialmente. En estos centros se enseñan lenguas extranjeras: alemán, árabe, chino, danés, francés, griego, inglés, italiano, japonés, holandés, portugués, rumano, ruso y español para extranjeros.

España cuenta en la actualidad con 87 Escuelas Oficiales de Idiomas, situadas por todo el país, en las que estudian más de 150.000 alumnos. Las lenguas con mayor demanda son inglés, francés y alemán. Sin embargo, en los últimos años, idiomas como el portugués, el árabe y el chino han crecido en popularidad.

(Adaptado de Hernández Cánovas, Isabel, y Kennedy, Bob, «Escuelas de idiomas», *Tecla*, University of London / Embajada de España, Londres, 1996, no. 30)

Actividad 2.6

Imagine that you want to enrol on a course similar to the one that Omar has chosen. Complete the letter opposite, addressed to the *Escuela Oficial de Idiomas*. Fill in the gaps with *ser* or *estar*, giving the correct form in the **present tense**. When only one verb is suggested, give the **perfect tense** of the verb.

Imagine que quiere matricularse en un curso similar al de Omar. Complete la siguiente carta dirigida a la Escuela Oficial de Idiomas.

Writing business letters

You are about to see an example of a formal letter written in Spanish. You might want to collect examples of different styles used in writing business letters. For example, you could take notes on how to write the date, the opening, the closing and the farewell in various types of letter, and keep them for reference.

Escuela Oficial de Idiomas
c/ Cisneros, 74
39007 Santander

8 de noviembre de 1998

Estimados señores:

Me dirijo a ustedes para pedirles información sobre sus cursos. (estudiar)...... ...... español durante cinco años y (ser/estar) ...... muy interesada en la cultura de su país. (visitar)...... ...... España en varias ocasiones, pero sólo (ir) .... de turista. Recientemente, mi jefe me (ofrecer) .... la posibilidad de trabajar en Madrid durante unos meses. Creo que (ser/estar)...... muy importante conocer la cultura del país para estar bien integrada. (ver)...... ...... en la Internet que ustedes ofrecen cursos de cultura española y (pensar) .... que (ser/estar) ...... ideales para mí. Les agradecería que me mandaran información sobre la matrícula.

Muchas gracias de antemano.

Atentamente,

Sección 2

This *sección* looks at communications and how new technologies have been integrated in different countries. You are going to be asked what you think of them.

Key learning points

- Describing and comparing objects
- Using the prepositions *para* and *en*
- Pronouncing *c* and *ch*
- Study skills: reading for gist

Actividad 2.7

Look at the illustrations of items that people use to communicate with each other. Match the numbers in the pictures with the vocabulary below.

Mire estos objetos que se usan para comunicarse con los demás. Una los números de los dibujos con los nombres.

Ordenador / Computador/Computadora   **Teléfono móvil**   **Buzón y carta**

---

la pantalla, el ratón, el cable, el sello, el botón,
el auricular, el módem, la antena, el sobre, el enchufe,
el teclado, el altavoz, la dirección, el disquete, el buzón

Actividad 2.8

1 Here is an extract from an article about a certain piece of equipment. Although not mentioned by name, the subject of this report seems to be dangerous, since some countries have restricted its use. What is it?

El texto siguiente describe un objeto que no se menciona, y cuyo uso parece ser peligroso. Estos países han reglamentado así su uso. ¿Qué es?

Reading for gist

When reading a text it is not necessary to understand every word and phrase in order to get the gist. Look for clues or key words to work out the general meaning. Try this with the following passage.

busca
bleeper

> ESTADOS UNIDOS Las disposiciones son variables según el cine, el teatro, el hospital o el restaurante. En general se consideran 'basura europea' y no están bien vistos porque los que empezaron a llevarlos y utilizarlos en lugar de los 'buscas' fueron los traficantes de droga.
>
> ALEMANIA El país que más restricciones impone a su uso. No pueden llevarse a los hospitales, cines, restaurantes, conciertos, discursos inaugurales y conferencias de prensa.
>
> ITALIA Es quizás el país de Europa en el que está más extendido su uso. Sólo se prohíbe utilizarlo conduciendo. Hay un anuncio advirtiendo que su uso es malo para la pasta.
>
> GRAN BRETAÑA No está permitido en la mayoría de los restaurantes de lujo o clubes selectos. Su robo es el delito que más ha aumentado en el país: 500 a la semana.
>
> ESPAÑA No existe ley que limite su uso, excepto las de la cortesía, la buena educación y el sentido común.
>
> FRANCIA No se prohíbe su uso más que en lugares concretos, pero no existe una regulación general. Los hombres lo llevan en el cinturón y las mujeres en el bolso.

2 Now identify the correct countries.

Ahora identifique los países correctos.

Ejemplo
¿Dónde está prohibido usarlo en hospitales? **Alemania**

(a) ¿Dónde no existen leyes generales sobre su uso?

(b) ¿Dónde se usa más en Europa?

(c) ¿Dónde está más restringido su uso?

(d) ¿Dónde están mal vistos en general?

(e) ¿Dónde está prohibido usarlo cuando se conduce?

(f) ¿Dónde se roban a menudo?

(g) ¿Dónde se dice que es malo para un tipo de comida?

Not everybody likes new technologies or is, indeed, able to use them. Some people still prefer to use tried and tested traditional methods. Here is your chance to compare old with new.

Read the *Atando cabos* below and then go on to *Actividad 2.9*.

Atando cabos

Los comparativos

In English, the following are instances of the comparative:

> The mail is **more** economical **than** the telephone.

> The telephone is **less** personal **than** the post.

> Cards are **as** personal **as** letters.

In Spanish, comparative constructions with adjectives follow this pattern:

más moderno	**que**	=	**more** modern	**than**
menos moderno	**que**	=	**less** modern	**than**
tan moderno	**como**	=	**as** modern	**as**

Some adjectives have an irregular comparative form:

| *bueno* (good) | → | *mejor* (better) |
| *malo* (bad) | → | *peor* (worse) |

Actividad 2.9

Make comparisons between the following means of communication, using the adjectives in the box.

Compare ahora los siguientes objetos, usando los adjetivos con las estructuras de comparativo anteriores.

1 el teléfono / la carta

2 el correo electrónico / la carta

3 el ordenador / el teléfono móvil

rápido, -a	seguro, -a	económico, -a
moderno, -a	confidencial	lento, -a

Ejemplo

El correo electrónico es **más** moderno **que** la carta.

Pronunciation and spelling: *c* and *ch*

The letter *c* is pronounced in different ways in Spanish according to how it is combined with other letters:

- before the letters *e* or *i* (*certificado*, *cine*) *c* is soft, and is pronounced like the 'th' in 'theme' (in non-Castilian Spanish it is pronounced like the 's' in 'seam');

- before letters *a*, *o* and *u* (*casa*, *comida*, *cubierto*) it is pronounced like the 'c' in 'Canada';

- when *c* occurs in combination with *h* it forms a new sound (as in *cucaracha*, *chocolate*) which is similar to the 'ch' in 'chair'.

In Spanish, *ch* is always pronounced in the same way (unlike in English, where it can also be pronounced like a 'k', as in 'chemistry', 'choir' or 'school').

Note that *h* is mute in all other combinations: that is, when it is not following *c*.

Actividad 2.10

1 Look at the list of words below. In some words the letter *c* is hard, as in *casa*, and in others it is soft, as in *certificado*. Indicate the correct pronunciation in each case by ticking the appropriate boxes in the columns below. Check your answers by listening to the pronunciation on Extract 6 (part one) of the Activities Cassette. The first time you hear the words they will be pronounced in Castilian Spanish.

Mire la siguiente lista de palabras e indique a cuál de los dos sonidos de la letra 'c' corresponden.

	Hard	Soft		Hard	Soft
vecina	❏	❏	palacio	❏	❏
campo	❏	❏	conozco	❏	❏
caza	❏	❏	cien	❏	❏
Colombia	❏	❏	casa	❏	❏
cinco	❏	❏			

2 Now listen to the same words in Extract 6 (part two) of the Activities Cassette. Each word is pronounced twice, first with Castilian pronunciation and then in non-Castilian Spanish. Notice the different pronunciations.

Escuche las mismas palabras pronunciadas en la variante castellana y la no castellana.

3 Now listen to Extract 6 (part three) on the Activities Cassette, where the following words containing the sound *ch* are pronounced, and repeat them after the recording.

Escuche las siguientes palabras, las cuales contienen el sonido 'ch' y repítalas.

> chocolate, cuchara, cucaracha, chorizo, mechero, chufa

Actividad 2.11

Listen to the telephone conversations on Extract 7 (part one) of the Activities Cassette and do the oral exercises in part two.

Escuche las conversaciones telefónicas y practique hablar por teléfono.

In the following *Atando Cabos*, you will learn how to use prepositions of place and purpose when talking about means of communication.

Atando Cabos

Preposiciones 'para' y 'en'

Two of the most commonly used prepositions in Spanish are *para* and *en*.

1 *Para* generally indicates purpose, intent or direction, for example:

*... sellos **para** cartas a los países de la Unión Europea (UE).*	... stamps for letters to European Union (EU) countries.
*Este teléfono sólo es **para** llamadas internas.*	This telephone is for internal calls only.
*Éste es un módem **para** PCs.*	This is a PC modem.

2 *En* generally indicates position and location, as in:

*El teléfono móvil está **en** el coche.*	The mobile phone is in the car.
*Correos está **en** la Plaza de Cibeles.*	The Post Office headquarters is in the Plaza de Cibeles.

Actividad 2.12

Practise using these prepositions by forming sentences, using a phrase from each column of the table below and linking them with **either** *para* or *en*. There are various possibilities and you may use the same phrase in more than one sentence.

Haga frases tomando un elemento de cada columna: enlácelas con 'para' o 'en'.

Ejemplo

El ordenador puede servir **para** enviar mensajes mediante un módem.

El ordenador puede servir…   … la calle.

El teléfono móvil no vale…   … comunicarse por escrito.

El correo electrónico se usa…   … enviar mensajes mediante un módem.

Las cartas son…   … todo el mundo.

El teléfono es…   … comunicarse oralmente.

Hay teléfonos públicos…   … recibir mensajes escritos.

Actividad 2.13

The article below deals with one of the most revolutionary technological advances of the twentieth century: the Internet. The Net is used not only for communication but also as a way of disseminating information.

Read the article, using *en* or *para* to fill the gaps.

Complete el texto con una de estas dos preposiciones: 'en' o 'para'.

> Se calcula que actualmente, más de 30 millones de internautas viajan virtualmente desde sus ordenadores ...... encontrar un tesoro: la información. ...... España existen más de 230.000 usuarios de la Internet y la mayoría de ellos la usan ...... fines científicos y académicos.
>
> Sin duda, la magia de esta red ...... el usuario español, igual que ...... el resto, se encuentra ...... los servicios que ofrece. Debido a la juventud del servicio ...... nuestro país, España actúa ...... la Internet como una esponja: 'estamos aquí ...... chupar información, no ...... ofrecerla', reconoce Juan Antonio Esteban, gerente del proveedor Goya.

(Adaptado de Jiménez, Marimar, «Internautas españoles» en *El País Dominical*)

(Ballesta, Juan, *Cambio 16*, 14 de octubre 1996, no. 1298)

Sección 3

Although Toledo retains much of its sense of history, it keeps up with the times in all other ways. Traditional jobs such as those of postal workers have changed significantly. Women have become part of the work force; new technology has been introduced; mail is transported and delivered in new ways. Even the nature of the mail is different.

> **Key learning points**
> - Talking about postal services
> - Using the superlative
> - Using or omitting *a* with the direct object
> - Study skills: categorizing vocabulary

Actividad 2.14

1   Before you listen to Extract 3 on the Interviews Cassette, think about the tasks that a postal worker normally performs. Tick the boxes in the list below to show whether or not you think they have to carry out the activities listed. Do not check in the *Clave* yet.

Antes de escuchar la grabación, indique qué actividades cree usted que realizan los carteros.

(a) vaciar los buzones ❑

(b) clasificar cartas ❑

(c) empaquetar las cartas ❑

(d) repartir el correo ❑

(e) conducir la furgoneta de correos ❑

(f) levantarse temprano ❑

(g) trabajar por las tardes ❑

(h) trabajar los fines de semana ❑

(i) utilizar máquinas ❑

2   Now listen to Extract 3 on the Interviews Cassette and compare your answers with what Luis and Enrique say.

Escuche la Cinta de entrevistas y compare sus respuestas con lo que dicen Luis y Enrique.

Actividad 2.15

Now listen to Extract 4 on the Interviews Cassette. Opposite are five pairs of sentences. In each case, tick the one that matches what is said on the cassette.

Escuche el resto de la grabación y marque qué frase corresponde a lo que se dice en la cinta.

1   Luis y Enrique usan una cartera para llevar las cartas.   ❑
      Luis y Enrique usan un carrito para llevar las cartas.   ❑

2   Hay más mujeres que hombres en la profesión de cartero.   ❑
      Hay tantas mujeres como hombres en la profesión de cartero.   ❑

3   Las mujeres introdujeron el carrito para llevar las cartas.   ❑
      Los hombres introdujeron el carrito para llevar las cartas.   ❑

4   Enrique escribe muchas cartas.   ❑
      Enrique escribe pocas cartas.   ❑

5   La novia de Enrique siempre responde a sus cartas.   ❑
      La novia de Enrique nunca responde a sus cartas.   ❑

Actividad 2.16

1   Can you remember what Spanish words or expressions are used in Extract 3 and Extract 4 for the words in the list below? Listen once more if you can't remember them all.

   ¿Se acuerda de qué palabras o expresiones se usan en la grabación para las palabras que aparecen más abajo?

   (a) postman

   (b) mail (two different words)

   (c) letters

   (d) postbox

   (e) van

   (f) postal bag

   (g) trolley / little trolley

   (h) postcards

   (* The English terms sound more formal than the Spanish expression.)

   (i) fines, bills and court orders*

   (j) I stop writing

El funcionario de correos con su carrito

2 Now arrange the words you have identified into a mind-map, as in the diagram below. This is a very useful way of recording vocabulary. Remember to change the verbs to their infinitive form.

Ahora coloque las palabras que ha identificado en el siguiente diagrama y ponga los verbos en infinitivo.

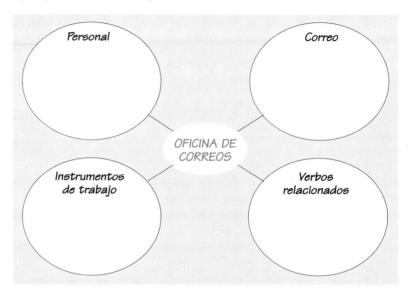

Atando cabos

El superlativo

Look at the following instances of superlative adjectives in English:

> The **nearest** postbox is by the **Town Hall**.

> The **busiest** time of the year for postal workers is Christmas.

In Spanish, superlatives are formed by adding *el, la, los, las* to the comparatives *más* and *menos*:

el buzón *más* cercano de aquí	the nearest postbox to here
la mujer *más* eficiente de correos	the most efficient woman in the post office
los sobres *más* caros de la tienda	the most expensive envelopes in the shop
las carteras de correos *más* pesadas	the heaviest postal bags

There are also some irregular forms:

el/la/lo mejor	the best
el/la/lo peor	the worst
el/la/lo mayor	the eldest / largest
el/la/lo menor	the youngest / smallest

Actividad 2.17

Practise the irregular superlatives by answering the questions below, using what you heard in the audio extract. Begin your sentences with the words in bold.

Practique los comparativos irregulares contestando las preguntas según lo que ha oído en la cinta.

1 ¿Qué cree Ud. que es **lo mejor de ser cartero**?

Lo mejor de ser cartero es…

2 ¿Qué cree Ud. que es **lo peor de ser cartero**?

3 ¿De qué se compone **la mayor parte del correo** que se reparte en la actualidad?

4 ¿De qué se compone **la menor parte del correo** que se reparte en la actualidad?

5 ¿Qué cree Ud. que **es mejor**, llamar por teléfono a los amigos o escribirles cartas?

Atando cabos

El objeto directo

A direct object is a noun or a pronoun that indicates what the verb is directly acting upon.

In the following sentence *el libro* is the **direct object** of the sentence:

*Miguel compra **un libro.*** Miguel buys **a book.**

Actividad 2.18

1 In Spanish, when the verb is followed by the direct object, the preposition *a* is sometimes needed. Compare the following sentences and try to work out the rule for using or omitting *a*.

Compare las siguientes frases y trate de deducir la regla para el uso o la omisión de 'a'.

(a) He visto **a** un amigo.

(b) Hoy he visto dos veces **a** tu padre.

(c) Escuchan atentamente **al** profesor.

(d) ¿Conocéis **a** Miguel?

(e) Ana va a visitar **a** sus abuelos.

(f) Teresa escribió **a** su madre.

(g) Vi **a** tu perro corriendo por el jardín.

(h) He visto un hombre.

(i) He visto dos veces esa película.

(j) Siempre escuchan la radio por las tardes.

(k) ¿Conocéis Toledo?

(l) Ana va a visitar la catedral de Toledo.

(m) Teresa escribió una carta muy larga.

(n) Vi un perro corriendo por el jardín.

2 Here are the rules. Which of the sentences in step 1 are governed by which of the three rules below?

Haga corresponder cada una de las frases anteriores con la regla apropiada.

- Personal *a* is required when the direct object of the verb is a named or specific person or animal.

- Personal *a* is **not** required when the direct object of the verb is an unidentified person or animal.

- Personal *a* is **not** required when the direct object of the verb is an inanimate object.

Note that the verb *querer* changes its meaning when it has a direct object with *a*.

Quiero un coche nuevo. — *I **want** a new car.*

Quiero **a** Andrés. — *I **love** Andrés.*

3 Now make up sentences by linking phrases from the left-hand column below with those from the right, using *a* when necessary.

Enlace las frases de la izquierda con las de la derecha: use 'a' cuando sea necesario.

He recogido…	… mi padre cuando entra en casa.
Miramos…	… la judería de Toledo.
Nunca oigo…	… Juan de arriba abajo.
¿Has visto…	… los niños del colegio.
Quieren visitar…	… mi libro por alguna parte?
Conoce…	… Susana desde que era una niña.

Actividad 2.19

Listen to a Colombian and a Spaniard speaking in Extract 8 of the Activities Cassette and practise the use of the personal *a*.

Escuche a una persona colombiana y a una española en el Extracto 8 en la Cinta de actividades y practique el uso del 'a' personal.

Categorizing vocabulary

It is important to remember the vocabulary you have learned. A useful way of doing so is by grouping words into categories, or organizing them thematically. You have had an example in this *unidad* of how to do this. Now try to do the same by revising the vocabulary from the last *unidad*, using other categories of your own such as words for describing people or places.

Resumiendo…

Now you can:

- talk about the recent past
- describe moods and character
- describe and compare objects
- pronounce *c* and *ch*
- use comparative and superlative adjectives correctly
- use *a* correctly to introduce personal direct objects

Unidad 3
Saludos, felicitaciones y despedidas

This *unidad* focuses on entertainment, what people do in their spare time and social relationships. The Audio Drama reveals more about Omar and Teresa's relationship as they go out and enjoy cultural life in Madrid. In *Sección 2,* you will find out about a favourite Spanish leisure activity, eating out. In *Sección 3*, you will listen to people from Toledo talking about their spare time activities and their social habits.

Sección 1

In the third episode of the Audio Drama, Teresa and Omar talk about what they like and dislike about the different places they visit. We shall then take a brief look at Spanish cinema. Finally, you will be asked what you like doing in your spare time.

Key learning points

- Expressing likes and dislikes

- Expressing opinions

- Using vocabulary relating to films

- Study skills: role-play

Actividad 3.1

1 What do you do at weekends? Tick those boxes that apply to you.

¿Qué hace los fines de semana? Marque las casillas correspondientes.

	nunca	casi nunca	a veces	con frecuencia	siempre
ir de compras				✓	
limpiar el coche					
arreglar el jardín					
ver la tele					
ir al campo					
ir al cine					
visitar a la familia					
salir a tomar una copa					
salir con los amigos					
estar sin hacer nada					
lavar la ropa					

2 Now use your answers to create sentences. Read them aloud. Remember to change the verbs in the first column to the first person. For instance, if you ticked *ir de compras* and *nunca*, you would say: *Nunca voy de compras.*

Ahora lea en voz alta lo que ha indicado en el cuadro. Acuérdese de cambiar los verbos de la primera columna a la primera persona.

Teresa and Omar visit many places together. In the next episode you will find out where they have been and what their impressions were.

Actividad 3.2

Listen to the first part of Episode 3 of the Audio Drama (up to '*¿Le importa que nos tuteemos? Claro, si tú quieres.*') and answer the following questions in English.

Escuche la primera parte del Episodio 3 del Radiodrama y conteste las siguientes preguntas en inglés.

1 Where are Teresa and Omar at the start of the episode?

2 What is the general mood of this scene?

As you will remember from *Unidad 1*, Teresa and Omar met for the first time when they were queuing for the cinema: they were going to see a film by the Spanish director Carlos Saura. In this episode they have been to see another film by another famous Spanish film director.

Actividad 3.3

1 What do you know about Spanish cinema? Can you answer the following questions?

¿Qué sabe del cine español? ¿Puede contestar las siguientes preguntas?

(a) ¿Puede nombrar tres películas españolas?

(b) ¿Conoce el nombre de tres directores o actores de cine españoles?

2 Here are the publicity blurbs for four films, taken from a Spanish entertainment guide. Read the blurbs and say which genre each film belongs to: *drama*, *suspense*, *terror* or *romántica*.

Lea las tres sinopsis de películas aparecidas en la 'Guía del Ocio'. Léalas y únalas a los géneros correspondientes.

La buena estrella. España 1997. Dir. Ricardo Franco. Un hombre mayor inicia una inesperada relación con una joven huérfana. El ex novio de la chica huérfana vuelve y se muda con la pareja: un triángulo amoroso nada convencional.

Memorias del ángel caído. España 1997. Los debutantes Fernando Cámara y David Alonso han empezado su carrera con una historia de zombies que vuelven a la vida después de ser envenenados.

Hazlo por mí. España 1997. Dir. Ángel Fernández Santos. La seducción y la manipulación son las claves de esta historia. Un ejecutivo aburrido es arrastrado a un mundo de delincuencia por una irresistible mujer.

Gracias por la propina. España 1997. Dir. Francesc Bellmunt. La infancia y la adolescencia de dos niños huérfanos criados en la Valencia de los años 60 se convierte en un canto a la tolerancia.

(Adaptado de la *Guía del Ocio* (*Especial Madrid*), noviembre 1997, no. 1144)

inesperado, -a
unexpected

huérfano, -a
orphan

una pareja
couple

envenenado, -a
poisoned

aburrido, -a
bored

es arrastrado, -a
(a)
is drawn (into)
(literally: dragged)

criado, -a
brought up

un canto
anthem, hymn

Actividad 3.4

1 Episode 3 of the Audio Drama mentions the names of four characters or people related to Spanish cinema. Listen to the episode again and write down their names and who they are.

Este episodio del Radiodrama menciona a cuatro personajes del cine español. Escuche la cinta y escriba quiénes son.

2 Look at this poster advertising a Spanish film and pick out all those words and expressions relating to cinema.

Mire el siguiente póster de una película española y busque el vocabulario relacionado con el mundo del cine.

(*El País*, 24 octubre 1997, p. 44)

A few weeks have elapsed and Teresa and Omar have been going out together. Omar has also met Teresa's daughter, Carmen. One day they decide to go to the Museo del Prado near the Parque del Retiro. As they are leaving they talk about the paintings they have seen.

Actividad 3.5

1 Listen to the second part of this episode (from '*Durante las siguientes semanas…*' up to '*A ti te estima.*') and answer the questions below.

Escuche la segunda parte del episodio y conteste las preguntas a continuación.

(a) ¿Le ha gustado el museo a Omar?

(b) ¿Qué pintor le ha gustado más?

(c) ¿Qué piensa Teresa de los cuadros de Goya sobre la guerra?

Atando cabos

El verbo 'gustar'

You have just heard Omar and Teresa talking about their likes and dislikes. The most common way of expressing likes and dislikes in Spanish is by using the verb *gustar*.

This verb uses a different construction from the English equivalent, 'to like'. Its literal meaning is 'to please' or 'to be pleasing to', as in:

Me gusta el arte.	I like art. ('Art is pleasing to me.')

Note that because of this construction, the verb agrees with what is pleasing: that is, in the following examples, *este cuadro* (this painting) or *los museos* (museums).

*Me gus**ta** **este cuadro.***	I like this painting.
*Me gus**tan** **los museos.***	I like museums.

In these two sentences, the pronoun *me* refers to the person who is being pleased. Other personal pronouns can be used similarly, as in:

***Te** gusta el Parque del Retiro.*	**You** like the Parque del Retiro.
***Le** gustan los cuadros de Picasso.*	**He/She** likes Picasso's paintings.
***Nos** gusta Miró.*	**We** like Miró.
***Os** gustan los cuadros alegres.*	**You** like lively paintings.
***Les** gusta el arte abstracto.*	**They** like abstract art.

When you want to say that you don't like something, you simply put *no* before the pronoun:

No *me gustan los museos.*	I don't like museums.
No *te gusta ir al museo.*	You don't like going to the museum.

¿Qué te parece?

Just as in English, there are many other ways in Spanish of expressing likes, dislikes and opinions. Some of them are common phrases such as *es impresionante* or *es una maravilla*. You have heard some of these in the Audio Drama.

Here are a few more phrases which express these feelings:

¡Es estupendo!	It's fantastic!
¡Es fenomenal!	It's great!
¡Está bien! / ¡No está mal!	It's OK! / It's not bad!
¡Me aburre! / ¡Es aburrido!	It bores me! / It's boring!
¡No lo soporto!	I can't stand it!

2   Now read the Audio Drama transcript. Note each line in which Omar expresses his reaction to the museum and its paintings. Then choose a phrase from the list above to replace his words. Find alternatives for each reaction and read them aloud. Do not forget to reflect the feelings in your intonation!

Ahora lea la transcripción y sustituya las frases que usa Omar por las diferentes frases para expresar opinión y gustos que le damos arriba.

Later in the episode, Omar and Teresa talk about Teresa's daughter, Carmen.

Actividad 3.6

1   Listen to the rest of the episode. Which three things are mentioned that Carmen does not like?

Escuche el resto de este episodio. ¿Qué tres cosas se mencionan que no le gustan a Carmen?

2   And you, what do you like? Write full sentences in Spanish contrasting what you like and what you do not like. Here are a few suggestions, but you can make up your own examples.

Y a usted, ¿qué le gusta más? Escriba frases diciendo lo que le gusta y lo que no le gusta.

Ejemplo

Me gusta la cerveza pero no me gusta el vino.

berberechos
cockles

(a) los berberechos / las aceitunas

(b) bailar la salsa / el rock

caracoles
snails

(c) la paella / los caracoles

(d) dormir la siesta / trabajar después de comer

(e) bañarse en la playa / bañarse en la piscina

Actividad 3.7

Now it's your turn to act the part of Omar or Teresa. Turn to the transcript of Episode 3 of the Audio Drama and read out the lines for your character. Try to speak at the same time as the actors. Do this a couple of times while reading the transcript, and then try to do it from memory.

Ahora va a hacer uno de los papeles del Radiodrama. Hable al mismo tiempo que el actor (o la actriz). Escuche y lea su parte un par de veces y luego intente hacerlo sin la transcripción.

Role-play

Playing the part of one of the characters in the Audio Drama will give you confidence in speaking Spanish. At the same time, you can memorize a few phrases that you will find useful later. Try to do this as often as you can.

Curiosidades~

¿'Tú' o 'usted'? En todos los idiomas, las fórmulas de tratamiento son importantes y contribuyen a hacer más fácil la convivencia diaria. En español es importante distinguir entre el 'tú', o tuteo, y el tratamiento de 'usted'.

ganar terreno
to gain ground

Antes, la mayoría de gente se dirigía a las personas mayores y a sus superiores de 'usted'. Pero las normas han cambiado en los últimos años. La sociedad española actual es más democrática, y el uso del 'tú' ha ganado terreno. Los alumnos ya no hablan de 'usted' a sus profesores ni los hijos a sus padres, como en el pasado. Pero aún hay que hablar de 'usted' a quien no se conoce, especialmente si es mayor o de clara superioridad en la jerarquía profesional. En cualquier situación, ante la duda, es mejor utilizar el 'usted'.

(Adaptado de Hernández Cánovas, Isabel, y Kennedy, Rob, «Tú o usted», *Tecla*, University of London / Embajada de España, Londres, 16 octubre 1995, no. 30)

Atando cabos

Letras mayúsculas

Capital letters are used less frequently in Spanish than in English. The two main differences in usage are given below. You should be able to complete the lists of examples given.

Capital letters are **not** used for:

- Months

enero	*febrero*	*marzo*
abril	• • • • • •	• • • • • •
• • • • • •	• • • • • •	• • • • • •
• • • • • •	• • • • • •	• • • • • •

- Days of the week

lunes	*martes*	• • • • • •	• • • • • •
• • • • • •	• • • • • •	• • • • • •	

- In films and book titles, capitals are used only for the first letter. For example:

El espíritu de la colmena	The Spirit of the Beehive
Lo que el viento se llevó	Gone with the Wind

However, capital letters are retained for proper names, as in the following film titles:

El crimen de Cuenca

Pepi, Luci, Boom y otras chicas del montón

Bienvenido Mr Marshall

Actividad 3.8

The sound /k/ may be spelled in three ways in Spanish: *c, k* or *qu*, as in *casa, kilo* and *quinto*.

The words in the list overleaf contain the sound /k/, but the spelling is incomplete. Complete each word, checking in the dictionary if necessary. As you do so, try to deduce a rule to explain why each is used.

Complete las siguientes palabras y trate de deducir las reglas de uso.

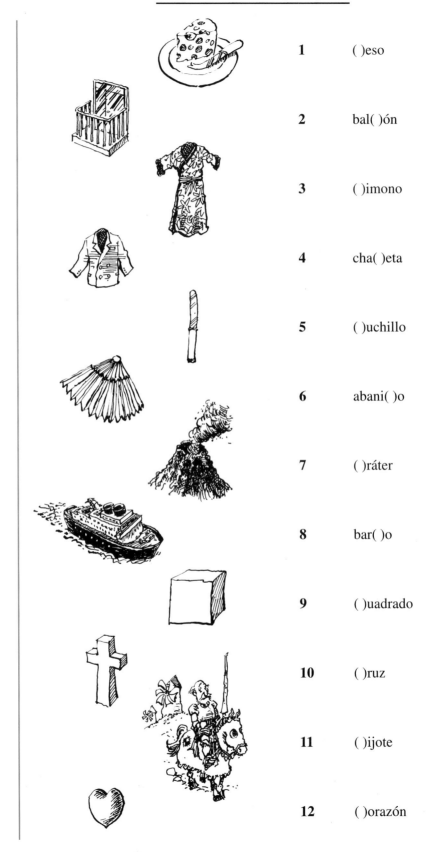

1   ( )eso

2   bal( )ón

3   ( )imono

4   cha( )eta

5   ( )uchillo

6   abani( )o

7   ( )ráter

8   bar( )o

9   ( )uadrado

10 ( )ruz

11 ( )ijote

12 ( )orazón

Sección 2

Madrid is a very lively city, both by day and by night. One of the favourite forms of entertainment for *madrileños* is going out for a meal. In this section you will find out about some of the best-known restaurants in Madrid. Finally, you will plan a trip to the surrounding countryside and cities, and finish your visit to the capital by going to a party.

Key learning points

- Making suggestions
- Accepting and declining offers (apologizing and giving excuses)
- Talking about the weather

Madrid offers a very varied choice of restaurants. You can find excellent Spanish, Castilian and international cuisine both in the centre of the city and in the surrounding districts. You don't need a special occasion to eat out. In fact, many people in Spain have their midday meals in a restaurant.

Actividad 3.9

1   Imagine that you have decided to go out for a meal in Madrid. Below are descriptions of a selection of restaurants and cafés, taken from a restaurant guide. First of all, read 'Your preferences' and then decide where you would like to go.

Aquí tiene una selección de algunos restaurantes en Madrid. Lea cuáles son sus preferencias y decida adónde le gustaría ir.

Your preferences

You fancy eating something typically *madrileño,* and in the open-air, if possible. You don't like fish. You would love to try the famous *cocido madrileño,* a dish made with meat and chick peas. You have only 3,000 pesetas to spend.

con gran solera
'a café with a lot of history and tradition'

finales de siglo
end of the century, fin-de-siècle

marisco
seafood

asado
roast

churrasco
large barbecued steak typical of Argentinian cuisine

a la parrilla
grilled

Café Gijón, Paseo Recoletos, 21. Café-restaurante con gran solera. Copia de los cafés de Buenos Aires de finales de siglo. Famoso por sus tertulias literarias. Cocina internacional. Se sirven tapas pero la especialidad es la paella. Tiene terraza en verano.

Casa Alberto, c/ Huertas, 18. Antigua taberna del siglo pasado. Especialidad en tapas de pescado y marisco. Precios de 1.500 a 3.000. Cerrado domingo noche y lunes.

La Pampa, c/ Amparo, 61. Un paraíso para los carnívoros. La especialidad de este restaurante son los platos de carne típicos argentinos: asado de tira, churrasco y carne a la parrilla. Tangos en vivo. Cerrado lunes. De 2.500 a 4.000.

aparcacoches
member of staff
responsible for
parking
cars

cocido
stew

Posada de la Villa, Cava Baja, 9. Cocina española y madrileña. Especialidad asados. Cerrado domingo noche. De 3.000 a 4.500 ptas. Aparcacoches.

Bola Taverna, Bola, 5. Cocina madrileña. Especialidad cocido, cocinado tradicionalmente. Sólo se sirve el cocido madrileño al mediodía. Se conserva la decoración antigua con azulejos. Cerrado domingo. No admite tarjetas. De 1.500 a 3.000 ptas.

La Plaza de Chamberí, en Pza. de Chamberí. Restaurante con terraza con comida moderna española. Buen ambiente. Cerrado domingo. Aprox. 2.500.

2   Now use the descriptions of the restaurants to help you match each suggestion with an appropriate answer. There are no 'right' answers because your choice will be subjective.

Ahora use las descripciones de los restaurantes para enlazar cada sugerencia con una respuesta apropiada.

(a) ¿Por qué no vamos al 'Café Gijón'?

(b) ¿Te apetece ir a 'Casa Alberto'?

(c) ¿Te apetece un restaurante argentino?

(d) ¿Quieres ir al restaurante 'Posada de la Villa'?

(e) ¿Te gustaría ir a la 'Bola Taverna'?

(f) ¿Te apetecería ir a 'La Plaza de Chamberí'?

(i) Sí, claro, parece que está muy bien de precio.

(ii) No, me gustaría algo típico madrileño.

(iii) Lo siento, no me apetece.

(iv) ¡Cómo no! ¡Me encantaría probar el cocido madrileño!

(v) ¡Estupendo! ¿Tiene aparcamiento?

(vi) Quizás, pero, ¿no es un poco caro?

3   Now listen to the same questions on Extract 9 of the Activities Cassette, and accept or decline the invitation as you did before.

Ahora escuche las mismas preguntas en la cinta, y acepte o rechace la invitación como acaba de hacer.

In some languages, the weather is a neutral topic for polite conversation. In Spanish, people usually talk about the weather for more practical reasons, such as planning a trip.

Actividad 3.10

1   You want to go on a trip out of Madrid this weekend, and you and your friend are wondering what the weather will be like. You have seen the weather map in the newspaper and are trying to choose where to go and what to do. Make a note of the weather in each location, and then suggest some appropriate activities from the list opposite.

Escoja las actividades apropiadas para cada lugar según el tiempo meteorológico.

	Tiempo	Actividad
Soria		
San Sebastián		
Sierra de Guadarrama		
Cuenca		

Actividades posibles

(una) cometa
kite

> tomar el sol, bañarse, salir a pasear, visitar un museo, hacer windsurf, pescar, hacer volar la cometa, tomar un helado, ir a un restaurante con terraza, jugar al tenis, quedarse en el hotel leyendo, hacer montañismo, ir de excursión

Now you are going to talk about the weather where you live.

 Está nublado

 Llueve

 Hace sol / Hace calor

 **Hace viento / Hace frío**

 Nieva / Hay nieve

2 A Spanish friend is planning to visit you – but only when the weather is good! He phones you to find out what the weather is like where you live in each season of the year. Prepare answers to the question *¿Qué tiempo hace…?* and say them aloud as if you were giving the reply by phone.

Un amigo español le llama para saber el tiempo que hace donde vive usted durante el año: prepare su respuesta y dígala en voz alta como si estuviera hablando por teléfono.

¿Qué tiempo hace en primavera?	¿Qué tiempo hace en otoño?
¿Qué tiempo hace en verano?	¿Qué tiempo hace en invierno?

Ejemplo

En primavera hace buen tiempo.

3 Listen to Extract 10 on the Activities Cassette. Listen to the aural clues and say what the weather is like.

Escuche la Cinta de actividades. Escuche los estímulos y diga qué tiempo hace.

So you've decided on your weekend destination, but before you leave Madrid you want to get to know some locals. The best way of doing this is probably by going to a social gathering or a *fiesta*. You are now going to learn a few expressions for these occasions.

Actividad 3.11

1 Somebody arrives at a party and is met by the hostess. Match each expression in the left column below with one from the right. Then listen to Extract 11 (part one), where you can hear the dialogue and check your answers.

Alguien llega a una fiesta y lo recibe la anfitriona. Enlace las siguientes expresiones de la columna de la izquierda con las de la columna de la derecha. Luego escuche la Cinta de actividades donde podrá escuchar el diálogo y comprobar sus respuestas.

Ejemplo

(a) – (vi)

(a)	Gracias por tu invitación.	(i)	Tú también vas muy elegante.
(b)	¡Qué guapo estás!	(ii)	Sí, gracias. ¡Qué ricos!
(c)	¿Quieres unos tacos de queso?	(iii)	Perdona.
(d)	¿Por qué no ponemos algo de música para bailar?	(iv)	¡Yo lo sé todo! ¡Feliz cumpleaños! ¿Bailamos?
(e)	¿Quieres bailar?	(v)	¡Qué buena idea!
(f)	¡Uy, qué daño! ¡Me has pisado!	(vi)	De nada.
(g)	¿Quieres otra copa?	(vii)	Lo siento, ahora no, quizás más tarde.

(h) Toma, para tu cumpleaños. ¡Felicidades!

(viii) No gracias, tengo que conducir.

(i) Pero… ¿cómo sabías que tenía tantos años?

(ix) ¡Qué detalle!

2 Now listen to Extract 11 (part two) of the Activities Cassette and react after the prompt, using appropriate expressions.

Escuche las expresiones en la cinta y reaccione.

Sección 3

If you were asked how sociable and pleasure-loving the Spanish are, what would you say? Do you think it is true that they love parties? In this *sección* you can read the result of a poll about what Spaniards do in their free time, and you will listen to some people being interviewed about their interests.

Key learning points
- Describing actions
- Talking about what you do in your spare time

Actividad 3.12

1 This chart shows what Spaniards like to do during their spare time. What is the most popular activity?

Este cuadro muestra qué hacen los españoles en su tiempo libre. ¿Cuál es la actividad más popular?

¿QUÉ HACEN EN SU TIEMPO LIBRE?

Pasear	27%	Ver la televisión	65%
Salir a bailar, ir a fiestas	3%	Hacer ejercicio, deportes	9%
Leer prensa, libros	24%	Salir con pareja / familia	17%
Reunirse con amigos	22%	Viajar, hacer excursiones	7%
Escuchar música	20%	Ir al cine	3%
Escuchar la radio (no música)	16%	Ir al teatro	1%
Hacer trabajos manuales	15%	Ir a espectáculos musicales	1%
Jugar con los hijos, atenderlos	13%	Ver alguna exposición	1%

(Encuesta del Centro de Investigaciones Sociales sobre los valores de los españoles.)

Cabos sueltos

Hablemos del tiempo libre

To talk about what you do in your spare time, you can make use of sentences like the following:

> **Me gusta** *leer novelas.*
>
> **Lo que me gusta más** *es hacer deporte.*
>
> **Mis hobbies preferidos** *son hacer excursiones y reunirme con mis amigos.*
>
> **Las actividades que practico** *son escuchar música y salir de excursión.*
>
> **Lo que más hago** *es ir al cine.*

2 Read the following questions and answer in Spanish.

Lea las siguientes preguntas y responda en español.

(a) ¿Qué actividad de la lista de la encuesta le gusta más?

(b) ¿Qué actividades de la lista de la encuesta hace usted?

(c) ¿Qué actividades que están en la lista de la encuesta no hace usted?

In Toledo, a journalist called Juan explains how Spaniards in general spend their free time, and how he himself would like to spend free time.

Actividad 3.13

1 First, look at the following list of activities and try to predict which ones Spanish people enjoy doing. Put a tick in the appropriate boxes but do not check the *Clave* yet.

Observe la siguiente lista de actividades y trate de predecir qué actividades se van a mencionar en la cinta. Marque los verbos en los recuadros correspondientes.

	Los españoles	Juan
beber en los bares	❑	❑
pasárselo bien	❑	❑
hacer deporte	❑	❑
ver la televisión	❑	❑
salir por la noche	❑	❑

conocer (chicas)	❏	❏
escuchar música	❏	❏
leer	❏	❏
salir por la calle	❏	❏
conocer gente	❏	❏
caminar por el campo	❏	❏
charlar	❏	❏
cocinar	❏	❏
buscar trabajo	❏	❏
jugar al fútbol	❏	❏
hacer puzzles	❏	❏
estar con otras personas	❏	❏
bailar	❏	❏

2 Now listen to the first question in Extract 5 on the Interviews Cassette and check your answers.

Escuche el Extracto 5 y compruebe sus predicciones.

3 Listen to the rest of Extract 5 and finish filling in the boxes by ticking those activities that Juan would like to do.

Escuche el Extracto 5 y complete la tabla marcando las actividades que a Juan le gustaría hacer.

Atando cabos

El gerundio

On the cassette you heard a few verbs that were not in the infinitive, but in a different form, the gerund. Here are a few examples:

*La gente en España se divierte **saliendo** por las noches.*

*La gente se divierte **bebiendo** en los bares.*

*La gente se divierte **saliendo** por la calle.*

*Hay gente que se divierte **yendo** al fútbol.*

*Hay gente que se divierte en casa **leyendo**.*

The gerund in Spanish corresponds to the '-ing' form in English (e.g. drinking, reading). The gerund of regular -ar verbs (*pasear, escuchar*) ends in *–ando*, while that of *–er* and *–ir* verbs (*beber, salir*) ends in *–iendo*, as in:

> *escuchando   saliendo   bebiendo*

There are just a few irregular forms, such as:

> *leyendo (leer)   cayendo (caer)*
>
> *durmiendo (dormir)   pidiendo (pedir)*
>
> *yendo (ir)*

Actividad 3.14

Listen to Extract 6 on the Interviews Cassette, where Juan tells us what he does at parties with friends and how he celebrates his birthday. Match the activities in the list opposite with the situations illustrated: a party with friends or a birthday with family and friends.

Escuche el Extracto 6 y decida a qué dibujo corresponde cada frase: una fiesta con amigos o un cumpleaños con familiares y amigos.

Una fiesta con amigos

Un cumpleaños en el pueblo con familiares y amigos

		Una fiesta con amigos	Un cumpleaños en el pueblo con familiares y amigos
1	Llevamos una botella de algo, o algo para picar.	❑	❑
2	Nos reunimos allí con una tarta.	❑	❑
3	Hablamos de cualquier cosa menos de trabajo.	❑	❑
4	Mi madre nos atiende a todos.	❑	❑
5	Me gusta reírme.	❑	❑
6	Nos sentimos muy felices.	❑	❑
7	Me gusta contar chistes.	❑	❑
8	Me gusta charlar con la gente.	❑	❑
9	Me tiran de las orejas.	❑	❑
10	Me gusta contar anécdotas del día.	❑	❑
11	Me dan regalos pequeños.	❑	❑
12	Me gusta hablar de mujeres.	❑	❑

Atando cabos

Describir lo que se hace

The way to express continuous action or ongoing events in Spanish is exactly the same as in English, by using

> estar + gerundio.

That is, by using estar (past, present or future form) together with the gerund of the verb for the activity.

Estoy leyendo un libro.	I **am reading** a book.
¿Estás escuchando?	**Are** you **listening?**
Está durmiendo.	She/he **is sleeping.**

Actividad 3.15

1 Look at the drawing below and write a short description of what the different subjects are doing. Use *estar* + the gerund form of the verbs listed.

Ahora mire el cuadro y describa lo que pasa usando la forma del gerundio y los verbos en la lista.

charlar, contar (una historia), escuchar, beber, limpiar, pintar

Actividad 3.16

Crucigrama

HORIZONTALES

3 Estación del año entre invierno y verano

5 Período de descanso del trabajo

8 Rito para dar nombre a un nuevo cristiano

10 Precipitación de las nubes en forma de gotas de agua

11 Instrumento mecánico o electrónico para mostrar la hora

VERTICALES

1 Utensilio portátil de mano que usamos cuando llueve

2 Último mes del año

4 Período central del día

6 Librito donde apuntamos los acontecimientos diarios, citas, notas, etc.

7 Una de las doce partes que tiene un año

9 Primer mes del verano

Resumiendo...

Now you can:

- express likes, dislikes and opinions
- talk about the weather
- pronounce and spell the sound /k/
- make suggestions
- accept and decline offers
- describe what somebody is doing
- talk about what you do in your free time
- use vocabulary relating to films

Unidad 4 *Puente aéreo*

The theme of this *unidad* is travel. In this episode of the Audio Drama you will hear how Teresa and Omar travel by train to Toledo to visit Teresa's mother. Next you will find out about different means of transport in Spanish America and practise making travel arrangements, in this case to go to Mexico. Finally, you will visit Madrid Barajas airport and hear about the journeys that different travellers are about to make.

Sección 1

In the fourth episode of the Audio Drama, Teresa announces to her mother, Doña Amelia, that she and Omar are planning to visit her in Toledo.

Key learning points

- Expressing the future with *ir a*
- Asking questions
- Using interrogative pronouns
- Study skills: selective listening; shadowing

Actividad 4.1

Listen to Episode 4 of the Audio Drama and answer the questions below in English.

Escuche el Episodio 4 del Radiodrama y conteste las preguntas en inglés.

Selective listening

Whenever you listen to the Audio Drama or an extract, you don't need to understand the whole passage. Try to concentrate simply on the information that interests you, or that you have been asked to listen for. Ignore what you don't need.

1 Who phones whom?

2 Is Doña Amelia pleased that Teresa is coming to visit her?

3 Has Teresa's mother met Omar before?

4 Where does the second part of the episode take place?

Asking for information is one of the most important skills you need to acquire. In the following *Atando cabos*, you will revise the so-called 'question words', or interrogative pronouns, that you need to formulate questions. The topic area here is making travel arrangements.

Atando cabos

Pronombres interrogativos

The most common interrogative pronouns in Spanish are:

qué	quién	cómo	por qué
dónde	cuándo	cuánto(s) / cuánta(s)	

They can be used in sentences such as the following:

¿**Qué** autobuses pasan por aquí?	Which buses come this way?
¿**Quién** va a Cuzco?	Who is going to Cuzco?
¿**Dónde** para el autobús?	Where does the bus stop? (Where do I catch the bus?)
¿**Cuándo** sale el próximo tren?	What time does the next train leave?
¿**Cómo** se va a Aranjuez?	What is the best way to get to Aranjuez?
¿**Por qué** no vamos en metro?	Why don't we take the underground?
¿**Cuánto** cuesta un billete de ida y vuelta?	How much is a return ticket?
¿**Cuántas** maletas lleva?	How many bags do you have?

73

Note that you can put a preposition before any of these interrogative pronouns:

*¿**Por dónde** se va a la estación?*	Which way is it to the station?
*¿**A cuántos** kilómetros está Madrid de Toledo?*	How many kilometres is it from Madrid to Toledo?
*¿**Para qué** van Teresa y Omar a Toledo?*	Why (for what purpose) are Teresa and Omar going to Toledo?
*¿**En qué** van Teresa y Omar a Toledo?*	How are Teresa and Omar getting to Toledo?

Remember that:

- Question marks are written both at the beginning and at the end of the question in Spanish: ¿…?

- *¿Por qué?* is written as two words when it is in a question, and as one word, *porque,* when introducing an answer. (*Me voy a Toledo **porque** me han dicho que es una ciudad muy interesante.*)

Actividad 4.2

The list of answers given below summarizes what happens in Episode 4 of the Audio Drama. Write down what you think the questions are.

Las siguientes respuestas resumen lo que pasa en el Episodio 4 del Radiodrama. Escriba las preguntas.

Ejemplo

Teresa llama a su madre.   ¿A quién llama Teresa?

1   El sábado por la mañana (Teresa va a Toledo).   ......

2   Es Omar quien va a Toledo con Teresa.   ......

3   Omar es de Marruecos.   ......

4   A las ocho y media (tren para Toledo).   ......

5   Porque el billete de ida y vuelta sale más barato.   ......

6   El viaje dura dos horas.   ......

You are going to listen to the first part of the episode once more. Notice that when the characters express intention, they use *ir a*. However, before you listen again, read the following grammatical explanation.

Atando cabos

'Ir a' + infinitivo

The use of *ir a* together with the infinitive is similar to English:

      ir a...   to be going to... (do something)

It is often used to describe a future action which has been planned:

      Miguel **va a** viajar en barco.

      ¿**Vais a** venir con nosotros a México?

      Eugenia y Pedro **van a** comprar los billetes de tren.

      Voy a buscar a mi hermana al aeropuerto.

      Voy a hacer un viaje a América en enero.

Actividad 4.3

1   Now listen to Episode 4 again (up to the second time the narrator speaks). You should hear the construction *ir a* used six times, followed by different verbs in the infinitive. Who says what?

Escuche la primera parte del Episodio 4 otra vez. El verbo 'ir a' seguido de otros verbos se usa seis veces. ¿Quién dice y qué se dice cada vez?

2   What are your plans for next weekend? Make up five full sentences in Spanish, using the construction *ir a*.

¿Qué planes tiene para el próximo fin de semana? Construya cinco oraciones en español usando la estructura 'ir a'.

Actividad 4.4

Listen to the second part of Episode 4, from *'Teresa está enfadada por la actitud de su madre'* to the end, and say whether the statements below are true or false.

Escuche la segunda parte del episodio y diga si las frases que siguen son verdaderas o falsas.

		Verdadero	Falso
1	Teresa y Omar van temprano a la estación.	❏	❏
2	Los trenes de Madrid a Toledo no salen con mucha regularidad.	❏	❏
3	Teresa y Omar ya tienen sus billetes.	❏	❏
4	Los billetes de ida y vuelta resultan más baratos.	❏	❏
5	El viaje de Madrid a Toledo dura tres horas.	❏	❏

6 La madre de Teresa vive cerca de la estación. ❏ ❏

7 Omar y Teresa se van a dar un paseo. ❏ ❏

8 Teresa cree que su madre no está en casa. ❏ ❏

Pronunciación y entonación: la entonación de las frases interrogativas

In Spanish, the voice usually drops at the end of questions. In the following examples, the direction of the pitch at the end of the sentence is indicated:

¿A qué hora sale el tren para Toledo? ↓

¿Cuándo vienes? ↓

However, the pattern may change according to the expected answer. For instance, the voice rises when expressing surprise or when the question requires a yes/no answer. This is particularly noticeable in sentences that could also be statements, such as:

¿Novio? ↑

¿Eres Teresa? ↑

¿Viene también Carmen? ↑

Actividad 4.5

1 In the fourth episode of *El idioma del amor*, all three characters ask each other questions. Did you notice the intonation pattern? Listen to the episode again (up to the second time the narrator speaks) and concentrate on this feature. Then repeat each question.

Escuche el episodio de nuevo y concéntrese en la entonación de las preguntas. Después repita cada pregunta.

Shadowing

You can improve your Spanish pronunciation by imitating the intonation of native speakers. Concentrating on the rising and falling patterns (the inflections) of the voice and trying to imitate the way they speak is a good way of practising.

Sección 2

Carmen and her aunt Mercedes are making plans to go to Mexico. Carmen tells us about what she intends to do there and Mercedes buys a ticket to go to Acapulco.

Key learning points

- Making travel plans
- Using the right prepositions for talking about travelling
- Pronouncing and spelling: *j* and *g*
- Study skills: memorizing set phrases

Actividad 4.6

1 Look at the cartoons below. Carmen is thinking about what she is going to do when she goes on holiday to Mexico with her aunt Mercedes. Try to put her thoughts into words in Spanish, using *ir a*. Below are a few words and expressions that will be useful.

Observe las viñetas. Carmen está pensando en lo que va a hacer cuando vaya a México de vacaciones con su tía Mercedes. Intente escribir frases en español sobre lo que está pensando.

nadar en el mar, leer en la playa, jugar a la pelota, hacer turismo, hacer fotos

Ejemplo

Vamos a nadar en el mar.

(a) (b) (c) (d)

2 Now what are **you** going to do?

Ahora, ¿qué va a hacer usted?

Curiosidades~

En Hispanoamérica el autobús
es más popular que el tren.
Los trenes son más baratos, pero hay
pocas redes ferroviarias y las pocas que hay
no son muy fiables. Encontrar asiento no es fácil si no se reserva con
antelación. En cambio, hay muchísimas clases de autobuses y autocares: de
lujo, antiguos, de cortas y de largas distancias. Éstos
tienen diferentes nombres en diferentes países:
por ejemplo en Cuba el autobús se llama 'la guagua',
en México 'el camión' o 'el pullman' si es de largas
distancias y de lujo, y en Argentina se llama
'el colectivo'.

red ferroviaria
railway network

fiable
reliable

autocar
coach

Un autobús en Hispanoamérica

Actividad 4.7

1 Listen to Extract 12 (part one) on the Activities Cassette, in which
Carmen and Mercedes are talking about their flight to Mexico, and
answer the following questions.

Escuche el Extracto 12 y conteste las siguientes preguntas.

(a) ¿Quién va a viajar por primera vez en avión?

(b) ¿Es muy caro el viaje?

(c) ¿Qué día van a salir?

(d) ¿A qué hora van a llegar?

2 Fill in the gaps in the following sentences with the correct form of *ir a*.

Complete las siguientes frases con la forma correcta de 'ir a'.

(a) Teresa y Doña Amelia no...... viajar a México.

(b) El vuelo...... ser muy largo.

(c) ¿Qué día...... volar a México Carmen y Mercedes?

(d) ¿Cuánto...... costar?

(e) Yo no......ir a México.

3 In Extract 12 (part two) of the Activities Cassette there are some
incomplete sentences. Practise your speaking skills by finishing them.

*Practique sus destrezas orales completando las frases en la Cinta de
actividades.*

Actividad 4.8

1   Read the following dialogue, in which Mercedes is buying a plane ticket for Acapulco at the airport in Mexico City. Check that you understand all the questions the booking clerk asks.

Lea el diálogo y compruebe que entiende todas las preguntas que hace la empleada de la taquilla.

Empleada ¿Qué desea?

Mercedes Un pasaje para Acapulco.

Empleada ¿De ida sólo o de ida y vuelta?

Mercedes De ida y vuelta.

Empleada ¿Paga en efectivo o con tarjeta?

Mercedes Con tarjeta.

Empleada ¿Viaja con alguien?

Mercedes Sí, con otra persona.

Empleada ¿Cuántas maletas llevan?

Mercedes Tres.

Empleada ¿Han hecho la maleta Uds. mismas?

Mercedes Sí.

Empleada ¿No han dejado las maletas desatendidas en ningún momento?

Mercedes No.

Empleada ¿Llevan algún aparato eléctrico?

Mercedes Sí, un secador.

Empleada ¿Desean asiento de fumador o no fumador?

Mercedes No fumador.

Empleada ¿Quieren ventanilla o pasillo?

Mercedes Un asiento de ventanilla y uno de pasillo, si es posible.

Empleada ¡Cómo no! Aquí tiene su billete y tarjeta de embarque. Su vuelo embarca por la puerta 23 en una hora. Gracias.

Mercedes Muchas gracias.

pasaje
(SpAm) plane or train ticket

pagar en efectivo or *en metálico*
to pay cash
pagar con tarjeta
to pay with a (credit) card

Memorizing set phrases

When you begin learning a language it can be useful to learn phrases by heart, especially when you are asking for specific information and the answers are quite predictable. By learning and practising these phrases, you will learn how to react in certain situations. In the following dialogue/exercise the questions and answers are very predictable, so you should have no difficulty in finding the right answer.

2 Now listen to Extract 13 on the Activities Cassette and take the part of Mercedes by responding to the questions the booking clerk asks you.

Escuche el Extracto 13 en la Cinta de actividades y haga el papel de Mercedes contestando las preguntas de la empleada.

When discussing travel arrangements, you need to talk about where you are going, how, when and with whom. The following *Atando cabos* deals with the prepositions you need for this.

Atando cabos

Preposiciones

Here are some prepositions you will need when talking about travelling. The most common are those indicating movement, position and time. But we will also see others. Here are a few examples:

Going towards something: use *a, hasta* or *para*:

> *a* (to; indicating direction and destination):
>> *Vamos andando **a** la estación.*
>> *Carmen y Mercedes van **a** Cancún.*

> *hasta* (towards, as far as, until; indicating a limited period or space):
>> *El autocar no para **hasta** Barcelona.*
>> *Este tren sólo va **hasta** Guadalajara.*

> *para* (for, towards; indicating direction):
>> *El tren **para** Chihuahua no sale hasta las cuatro de la tarde.*
>> *Este camión va **para** el centro.*

Coming from: use *de*:

> *Julián es **de** Veracruz.*

> *Es el tren **de** cercanías.*

Movement within certain limits (through): use *por*:

> *El vuelo con destino a México DF sale **por** la puerta 9.*

> *El camión pasa **por** la Avenida de la Reforma.*

Location in space: use *en:*

> *Los servicios se encuentran **en** la vía.*
>
> *El vagón coche cama está **en** la parte delantera del tren.*
>
> *El pasaje de avión está **en** la mesa / **en** el cajón.*

Location in time (for, towards): is indicated by *hasta, a, para* and *por:*

> *El vuelo de Buenos Aires llegará **a** las dos de la tarde.*
>
> *El pullman no sale **hasta** las nueve.*
>
> *El tren llegará **para** las diez.*
>
> *Voy a Argentina **por** un par de meses.*

Showing who you are with: use *con:*

> *Carmen va a México **con** Mercedes.*
>
> *¿**Con** quién viajas?*

Actividad 4.9

Fill the gaps in the following description of Carmen's trip with the prepositions listed above.

Complete la siguiente descripción del viaje de Carmen con las preposiciones mencionadas más arriba.

> Este año, Carmen va a ir ...... México de vacaciones ...... dos semanas. No va sola: va ...... su tía. Siempre ha querido ir a México. Su avión sale ...... Madrid y no hace escala en ninguna parte. Vuela directo ...... México. Allí Carmen y su tía Mercedes van a alojarse ...... un hotel...... cinco días. Han alquilado un coche y van a viajar ...... todo el país, así que...... el día que tienen que regresar...... España, van a visitar los lugares que Carmen siempre ha deseado conocer.

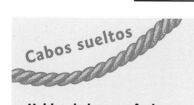

Hablar de horas y fechas

¿Qué hora es?

Son las tres (en punto).

Son las ocho menos cuarto.

Son las doce y media.

Son las cinco y diez.

Es la una y cuarto.

Son las siete menos veinticinco.

Durante el día...

Por la mañana

Al mediodía

Por la tarde

Por la noche

fue
past tense of *ser*:
'it was'

será
future tense of *ser*:
'it will be'

Día tras día…

Hoy es el 7 de julio. Ayer fue el 6 de julio. Mañana será el 8 de julio y pasado mañana será el 9 de julio. Dentro de una semana, me voy de vacaciones. Vuelvo el mes que viene, en agosto.

Actividad 4.10

Carmen is going to have a very busy couple of days before she goes on holiday.

Look at the notes that she has made on her calendar. Then, using *ir a*, write sentences about what she is going to do.

Mire las anotaciones que ha hecho en su calendario y escriba frases sobre lo que va a hacer.

Ejemplo

El martes a la una y media Carmen va a comer con Elisa.

Pronunciación y ortografía (*g* y *j*)

In Castilian Spanish, the letters *g* (when followed by *e* or *i*) and *j* are pronounced in a different way from English. The sound is similar to the 'ch' in the Scottish 'loch'.

In non-Castilian Spanish, however, *g* and *j* are pronounced like the English 'h'.

When this sound is followed by *e* or *i*, the word might be spelled with either *j* or *g*. In this case the spelling has to be learned, for example:

    via**je**   **ji**rafa   tar**je**ta

    gitano   **ge**neral

When followed by *a*, *o* or *u*, it is always spelled with *j*:

    jarabe   co**jo**   **Ju**lia

To sum up:

    j always has this sound and can be followed by *a*, *e*, *i*, *o*, *u*, or appear at the end of a word (as in *reloj*).

    g only has this sound when followed by *e* or *i*.

Actividad 4.11

1   Listen to Extract 14 on the Activities Cassette and repeat the words as they are pronounced.

    Escuche el Extracto 14 en la Cinta de actividades y repita las palabras.

2   Listen to the extract once more, write the words down and check the *Clave*. Did you spell them correctly?

    Escuche las palabras otra vez y escríbalas. ¿Las ha escrito correctamente?

Sección 3

You are now at Madrid's airport, Madrid Barajas, the busiest in Spain. Two people are interviewed about the trips they are about to undertake.

Key learning points

- Revising the prepositions *por, en* and *con*
- Saying 'no' with *no* and *nunca*
- Extending vocabulary relating to travelling

Actividad 4.12

Look at this picture of an airport terminal and link the figures labelled with the words and expressions in the box.

Mire el dibujo y una las letras con el vocabulario siguiente.

> cinta transportadora de equipajes, salidas, carrito, monitor, mostrador de facturación, tienda libre de impuestos, pasajero, maleta, control de seguridad, llegadas

Curiosidades~

civil
civilian

facturar
to check in

mostrador
check-in desk

En España cada vez hay más aeropuertos y líneas aéreas. Hoy en día hay treinta y cuatro aeropuertos entre los militares y los civiles. Los aeropuertos más importantes son el de Barajas en Madrid y el Prat en Barcelona. Miles de pasajeros de todo el mundo facturan a diario en los mostradores de estos aeropuertos con destino a otras ciudades españolas, americanas y europeas. Todo empezó en 1927 con la explotación de la línea Madrid–Barcelona. Ahora a este servicio se le llama 'Puente Aéreo'. Más adelante, en 1946, la compañía aérea Iberia empezó a volar a América del Sur con vuelos regulares a Buenos Aires.

Next you are going to listen to two people who are just setting off from Barajas airport. But first, try to predict what they will say.

Actividad 4.13

1 Write five questions in Spanish that you might ask people who are waiting for their flights to be announced.

Escriba cinco preguntas que se le pueden hacer a una persona que espera a que anuncien su vuelo.

Ejemplo

¿A qué hora sale su vuelo?

2 Now listen to Extract 8 and Extract 9 on the Interviews Cassette and note below which of the following statements refer to which of the two people interviewed.

Escuche los Extractos 8 y 9 de la Cinta de entrevistas y marque a continuación a quién de las dos personas entrevistadas corresponden las siguientes afirmaciones.

	Carlos	María Elena
Viaja al continente americano.	❏	❏
Sabe por qué puerta sale su vuelo.	❏	❏
Hace escala en Europa.	❏	❏
Viaja solo(, -a).	❏	❏
Viaja por negocios.	❏	❏
Le gusta leer en el avión.	❏	❏
Lleva dos maletas.	❏	❏
Viaja con su hijo.	❏	❏
Ha viajado por todo el mundo.	❏	❏
Su vuelo tarda ocho horas.	❏	❏

Now you are going to listen to Carlos again.

Actividad 4.14

Listen to Extract 8 on the Interviews Cassette again and match the expressions on the left with the corresponding phrase in the right-hand column. If you are not sure, check with the transcript.

Escuche el Extracto 8 otra vez y enlace las expresiones de la columna de la izquierda con las expresiones de la columna de la derecha.

(a) la duración del vuelo

(b) el motivo de su viaje

(c) lo que le gusta hacer en el avión

(d) los ha visitado

(e) el lugar de la escala

(f) los medios de transporte que no ha utilizado

(g) las personas con quienes viaja

(h) la duración de su estancia

(i) su equipaje

(j) la hora de salida de su vuelo

(k) el destino de su vuelo

(i) Toronto

(ii) más de cincuenta países

(iii) negocios

(iv) a la una, más o menos

(v) cinco, seis horas

(vi) París

(vii) compañeros de trabajo

(viii) tres o cuatro semanas

(ix) dos maletas

(x) leer

(xi) globo aerostático y submarino

Actividad 4.15

César Cardeñoso is waiting in Toronto for Carlos to arrive from Madrid. Read the fax he has just received and fill in the gaps, using expressions from the box below, together with the correct forms of the verbs.

César Cardeñoso está esperando en Toronto a Carlos que viene de Madrid. Lea el fax que acaba de recibir y complete el texto con las palabras y expresiones del recuadro.

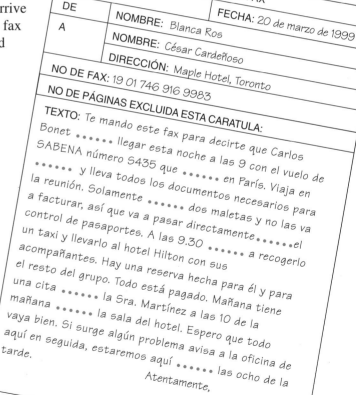

TELEFAX

FECHA: 20 de marzo de 1999

DE

NOMBRE: Blanca Ros

A

NOMBRE: César Cardeñoso

DIRECCIÓN: Maple Hotel, Toronto

NO DE FAX: 19 01 746 916 9983

NO DE PÁGINAS EXCLUIDA ESTA CARATULA:

TEXTO: Te mando este fax para decirte que Carlos Bonet •••••• llegar esta noche a las 9 con el vuelo de SABENA número S435 que •••••• en París. Viaja en •••••• y lleva todos los documentos necesarios para la reunión. Solamente •••••• dos maletas y no las va a facturar, así que va a pasar directamente •••••• el control de pasaportes. A las 9.30 •••••• a recogerlo un taxi y llevarlo al hotel Hilton con sus acompañantes. Hay una reserva hecha para él y para el resto del grupo. Todo está pagado. Mañana tiene una cita •••••• la Sra. Martínez a las 10 de la mañana •••••• la sala del hotel. Espero que todo vaya bien. Si surge algún problema avisa a la oficina de aquí en seguida, estaremos aquí •••••• las ocho de la tarde.

Atentamente,

Blanca

hacer escala, ir a, en, por, ir, hasta, primera clase, llevar, con

Actividad 4.16

Look at the illustration and listen to Extract 9 on the Interviews Cassette again. Take note of the three differences between what you see in the picture and what you hear on the cassette.

Mire el dibujo y escuche otra vez el Extracto 9 de la Cinta de entrevistas. Tome nota de las tres diferencias que existen entre el dibujo y lo que oye en la cinta.

Actividad 4.17

Now listen once more to Extract 9, and decide whether the statements below are true or false. Correct the false ones in Spanish.

Ahora escuche otra vez y decida si las siguientes frases son verdaderas o falsas. Corrija las que son falsas.

		Verdadero	Falso
1	María Elena viaja mucho por Europa.	❏	❏
2	Su avión sale a las tres menos cinco.	❏	❏
3	María Elena no sabe a qué hora sale su avión.	❏	❏
4	Su vuelo tarda más o menos nueve horas.	❏	❏
5	Su vuelo hace dos escalas: en Miami y El Salvador.	❏	❏
6	María Elena viaja sólo con su hijo.	❏	❏
7	No lleva mucho equipaje.	❏	❏
8	María Elena trata de mantener a su hijo despierto durante el vuelo.	❏	❏

Atando cabos

'No' y 'nunca'

To put a Spanish sentence into the negative, *no* is placed directly before the conjugated verb:

> *Juan **no** quiere ir en avión.*

Belén y Pablo todavía **no** han comprado los billetes.

No me gusta viajar.

Nunca means 'never'. It can follow the verb, and in this case also requires *no* in front of the verb:

No he ido **nunca** a Guatemala.

No los habéis visto **nunca**.

However, *nunca* may also come first in the sentence. In this case, *no* is not required:

Nunca he ido a Guatemala.	I have never been to Guatemala.
Nunca los habéis visto.	You have never seen them. (Never have you seen them.)

Actividad 4.18

1   The people interviewed talk about things that they have done and about their travel plans. To whom do each of the following sentences apply? Add the name in the last column below. If you cannot remember, refer to the transcript.

¿A quién se refieren las siguientes frases? Si no se acuerda, vaya a la transcripción.

Ejemplo

... reads on the plane.   Carlos

(a) ... has four pieces of luggage.   ......

(b) ... is on a business trip.   ......

(c) ... is travelling with his/her family.   ......

(d) ... says that s/he has never been on a submarine.   ......

(e) ... has visited over fifty countries.   ......

(f) ... is on a flight with a stopover in Miami.   ......

(g) ... is going to be flying for eight hours.   ......

2   Now form **negative** sentences in Spanish based on the sentences in step 1, using phrases and vocabulary given in *Atando cabos* above.

Ahora construya frases negativas en español basadas en las frases del paso 1. Use expresiones y vocabulario del 'Atando cabos'.

Ejemplo

(... reads on the plane.)   María Elena no lee en el avión.

Actividad 4.19

Here is a list of words and phrases, some appropriate to travel by air, some to travel by train and some to both. Write them in the appropriate spaces in the circles. Some have been done for you.

Escriba las siguientes palabras en el espacio adecuado.

billete, horario, tren, avión, terminal, pasaporte, maleta, ida y vuelta, carrito, viajar, reserva, asiento, tienda libre de impuestos, pasajero, azafata/o, andén, vías, fumador / no fumador, salir, llegar, estación, vagón, destino, vuelo regular, cercanías, hacer escala, ventanilla, mostrador de facturación, pasajes, revisor

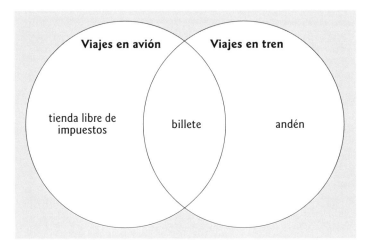

Viajes en avión   **Viajes en tren**

tienda libre de impuestos   billete   andén

Resumiendo...

Now you can:

- express the future with *ir a*

- ask questions

- make travel plans

- use prepositions to talk about travelling

- pronounce *j* and *g*

- say 'no', 'not' and 'never' using *no* and *nunca*

- use vocabulary relating to travelling

Unidad 5
La casa de los espíritus

In this episode of the Audio Drama, Teresa and Omar are going to visit Doña Amelia in Toledo. You will find out how they get on.

Continuing the theme of homes and houses, some people from Toledo are interviewed on the Interviews Cassette. This will give you an impression of what houses in Toledo are like now and what they were like in the past. You will learn the characteristics of a 'typical' Toledan house and find out how past cultures have left their mark on the architecture.

Sección 1

In Episode 5 of the Audio Drama, Omar and Teresa visit Teresa's mother in Toledo, but Doña Amelia is not content with merely being introduced to Omar.

Key learning points

- Describing houses and flats
- Putting adjectives in the correct position
- Pronouncing *ll*, *y* and *ñ*

Actividad 5.1

1 Before you listen to Episode 5, look at the illustrations below and decide which names represent objects you are likely to find in a home. Which room are you most likely to find them in? Write the names of these objects beneath the name of the appropriate room.

Antes de escuchar el Episodio 5, mire el dibujo y decida qué objetos encontraría en una casa. Escriba los nombres de los objetos en la habitación más apropiada.

2 Can you think of any more words for describing the parts of a house and its contents? Make a list of all those you can remember.

¿Se acuerda de otras palabras para describir las partes de la casa y sus contenidos? Haga una lista de todas las que se acuerde.

Showing visitors round your home on their first visit is a very Spanish custom. Unfortunately, Omar's visit to Teresa's mother's home does not end very well!

Actividad 5.2

Listen to Episode 5 of the Audio Drama, up to '*... me gusta mucho.*' Decide whether the statements below are true or false, and correct the false ones according to what you hear on the cassette.

Escuche el Episodio 5 del Radiodrama. Decida cuáles de las siguientes afirmaciones son correctas, y corrija las que son falsas según la cinta.

		Verdadero	Falso
1	La madre y Omar se besan.	❏	❏
2	La madre se va al baño.	❏	❏
3	Teresa y Omar se sientan a hablar.	❏	❏
4	A Omar le gusta la casa.	❏	❏

Actividad 5.3

Listen to the narrator describing the sitting room in Teresa's mother's home, from '*Los tres se dirigen al salón*' to '*... invita a Omar a que se siente*' and say which of the three pictures below and overleaf matches the description.

Escuche la descripción que hace el narrador del salón de la casa de la madre de Teresa y averigüe cuál de los tres dibujos corresponde a la descripción.

(a)

93

(b)

(c)

Finding a flat in Madrid is not an easy task. A good way to begin is by looking in newspapers under advertisement sections labelled *Inmobiliaria ventas y alquiler*.

Actividad 5.4

1 Read the newspaper cutting (right), advertising flats to let. Make a list of all the abbreviations you can find and write next to each, in Spanish, what you think they might mean.

Haga una lista de las abreviaciones que encuentre en el siguiente recorte de periódico y escriba lo que cree que significan.

INMOBILIARIA VENTAS Y ALQUILER

A Se alquila hab. en piso céntrico, coc. y baño a compartir. Ascensor y calefacc. central. Llamar al 2300987 de 6 a 9 de la noche.

B Bonito ático, con cocina, 3 hab., tza, baño y salón. Z. centro. Precio de venta a convenir. No hay ascensor. Tlf. 2323231.

C Alquilo apto., p. baja, 2 dormitorios amueblados. Baño. Cerca centro. 70.000 mes. Para más información, llamar al 3458002.

D Chalé amueblado, 80.000 pesetas alquiler, con gastos incluidos. Situado en las afueras, zona tranquila y bien comunicada con el centro. Llamar al 4566767 en horas laborales.

2 Choose a flat to rent from those on offer, according to the following list of your requirements.

Escoja un piso de alquiler de acuerdo con los siguientes requisitos.

- Zona céntrica.
- Máximo: 100.000 pesetas mes.
- Con cocina, 2 dormitorios mínimo, baño.
- Debe tener ascensor o ser planta baja.
- Amueblado o sin amueblar.

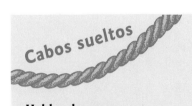

Hablar de casas

Se alquila.	To let.
Se vende.	For sale.
Es un piso comprado.	It's owner-occupied. / I own the flat.
Es un piso alquilado.	It's a rented flat.
Es una casa modesta.	It's a modest house.
Es una casa de lujo.	It's a luxury house.
Es un piso exterior.	It's a flat that looks out on to the street.
Es un piso que da al interior.	It's a flat that backs on to a courtyard.
Es céntrico.	It's central.
Está en las afueras.	It's on the outskirts.
Está amueblado / sin amueblar.	It's furnished / unfurnished.
Está bien / mal distribuido.	It is well / badly laid out.
Tiene jardín.	It has a garden.

Now look at *Atando cabos* for some more information on agreement and position of adjectives in Spanish sentences.

Atando cabos

La posición de los adjetivos

In *Unidad I* you learned how adjectives agree in gender and number with the noun or pronoun they describe, as in:

un armario abierto   *una puerta cerrada*

Now we are going to concentrate on their position in the sentence. Adjectives most frequently follow the noun they describe, as in:

un apartamento ordenado y limpio

Toledo es una ciudad interesantísima

Certain common masculine singular adjectives such as *bueno, malo, primero* and *tercero* may be used before the noun, but in this case they become shortened to *buen, mal, primer* and *tercer*:

un buen precio   *un mal aspecto*

el primer piso   *el tercer balcón*

Similarly, the adjective *grande* may also precede the noun. However, before a singular noun (masculine or feminine) it becomes *gran*:

la casa grande / la gran casa   *el salón grande / el gran salón*

but *casas grandes / grandes casas*

A few adjectives have two different meanings according to whether they are used before or after the noun:

una ciudad grande a large city   *una gran ciudad* a great city

---

Actividad 5.5

To practise the use of adjectives further, draw a line to link each noun in column A with one or more adjectives in column B, and then form phrases.

Una cada nombre con el adjetivo o adjetivos adecuados para formar frases.

A	B
unas ventanas	apagadas
un comedor	blancas
unas lámparas	oscura
un sillón	limpio
una habitación	anchas
unas cortinas	blando

In the spoken language it is sometimes difficult to distinguish words. This is because they are not separated by spaces and punctuation as in the written language: instead, words appear to run together. Pauses in the spoken language are used to separate sense, not words. In poetry this becomes even more apparent.

Actividad 5.6

1   Listen to Extract 15 on the Activities Cassette. This is an excerpt from a poem by the Spanish poet, Antonio Machado. Pay special attention to the way the words run together.

Escuche el poema y preste especial atención a cómo se juntan las palabras.

2   Listen to the poem again. This time concentrate on the pronunciation of the letters *ñ*, *ll* and *y*.

3   Now read the poem aloud in time with the cassette, and imitate the pronunciation.

Ahora lea el poema en voz alta al mismo tiempo que la cinta e imite la pronunciación.

La casa

La casa de Alvargonzález
era una casona vieja,
con cuatro estrechas ventanas,
separada de la aldea
cien pasos, y entre dos olmos
que, gigantes centinelas,
sombra le dan en verano,
y en el oto**ñ**o hojas secas.
Es casa de labradores,
gente aunque rica plebe**y**a,
donde el hogar humeante
con sus esca**ñ**os de piedra
se ve sin entrar, si tiene
abierta al campo la puerta. [...]

En una estancia que tiene
luz al huerto, hay una mesa
con gruesa tabla de roble,
dos si**ll**ones de vaqueta; [...]

Y era a**ll**í donde los padres
veían en primavera
el huerto en flor, **y** en el cielo
de mayo, azul, la cigüe**ñ**a [...]

(Machado, Antonio, «La tierra de Alvargonzález»
in *Poesías completas*, 1978, Espasa-Calpe SA, Madrid)

casona
great house, usually large and stately

aldea
small village, hamlet

el centinela
guard, sentry

labrador
farmer

hogar
fire-place, hearth

escaño
seat, bench

roble
oak

vaqueta
calfskin, leather

cigüeña
stork

Sección 2

In this *sección* you will look at housework and pick up some tips about environmentally friendly housekeeping. Meanwhile, in the Audio Drama, Carmen helps Teresa while Omar is at home doing various jobs.

Key learning points

- Giving orders
- Giving advice
- Using the imperative (*tú* and *vosotros* forms)
- Prepositions of place

First read *Atando cabos,* which deals with the informal imperative in Spanish. You are going to need it for the next activity.

Atando cabos

El imperativo informal

The imperative is widely used in Spanish. This form of the verb can be used for various purposes:

giving orders;	giving instructions;
giving advice;	requesting something.

Here, we are going to concentrate mainly on two uses, giving orders and advice. Look at the following examples:

order   **Sube** *la silla al piso de arriba.*

advice   **Lava** *los jerseys de lana con agua fría.*

The singular informal imperative (*tú*) is formed by taking the second person singular of the present tense and dropping the final *s*:

(*tú*) tomas	→	**toma**
(*tú*) comes	→	**come**
(*tú*) subes	→	**sube**

There are some irregular imperatives in the *tú* form:

salir	→	**sal**
tener	→	**ten**

poner	→	**pon**
venir	→	**ven**
decir	→	**di**
hacer	→	**haz**
ir	→	**ve**

The plural form is constructed from the infinitive, by replacing the *r* at the end with *d*.

toma(r)	→	(*vosotros*) **tomad**
come(r)	→	(*vosotros*) **comed**
subi(r)	→	(*vosotros*) **subid**

Note: for the time being you should concentrate only on these forms. The negative and the *usted* forms are produced differently.

Teresa and Carmen are tidying the kitchen, waiting for a visit from Omar.

Actividad 5.7

1 In the following dialogue, Teresa tells Carmen what to do. Put the verbs in brackets into the imperative form. (The only negative imperative you will need is *rompas*.)

Check your answers by listening to Extract 16 (part one) of the Activities Cassette.

Ponga los verbos entre paréntesis en el imperativo. Compruebe sus respuestas con la Cinta de actividades.

Teresa Carmen, por favor, (abrir) la ventana para ventilar la cocina. ¡Y (cerrar) la puerta, que pasa mucha corriente!

Carmen ¿Dónde quieres que ponga los vasos que están junto a la ventana?

Teresa (Poner) los (vasos) sobre el frigorífico, pero antes sécalos.

Carmen ¡Ay! Lo siento.

Teresa (Dejar) lo, ya lo recojo yo. Bueno, (llevar) las sillas al salón. Carmen, (abrir) la puerta, debe de ser Omar. ¡Ten cuidado… no (romper) el jarrón!

Carmen ¡Ay! ¡Lo siento mucho!

2 Now listen to Extract 16 (part two) and play the role of Teresa, reacting to the prompts in English.

Ahora haga el papel de Teresa en el Extracto 16: segunda parte.

Omar is also very anxious to see Teresa again. In the meantime he concentrates on household chores.

Actividad 5.8

1 Some of Omar's problems are listed below. Possible advice is given in brackets. Write complete sentences advising Omar.

Escriba frases para aconsejar a Omar.

Ejemplo

Estoy un poco nervioso.

(tomar una tila)

Toma una tila.

(a) No tengo las llaves.
(entrar por la ventana)

(b) No hay comida en la nevera.
(ir al supermercado)

(c) Tengo frío.
(poner la calefacción)

(d) Tengo la camisa sucia.
(poner la lavadora)

(e) No encuentro los pantalones vaqueros.
(buscar en la cómoda)

(f) Hay polvo sobre la mesa.
(pasar el trapo del polvo)

trapo
cloth, duster

polvo
dust

colada
the washing

(g) Va a llover.
(entrar la colada)

(h) Ya estoy listo.
(ir más temprano)

2 Look at the illustrations opposite, taken from a leaflet on how to be more environmentally minded in the home. Write seven tips for 'green' housekeeping by making up sentences using the words and phrases given. Remember to use the imperative form.

Construya siete frases con sugerencias para un cuidado de la casa ecológico.

comprar   vinagre, jabón o limón

limpiar   productos naturales

apagar   para gastar menos agua

rodearse   luces si no las usas

reciclar   comida sin envoltorio

ducharse   plantas en tu casa

usar   basura

Atando cabos

Más preposiciones

In the last unit you looked at prepositions useful for talking about travel. They represented movement (*a, hasta, para*); space (*en*); time (*a, hasta, para, por*); and who you are with (*con*). We shall now consider how to say exactly where something is located.

You have already met three expressions referring to location in the Audio Drama. *Al fondo, en el centro* and *enfrente* were used in describing Doña Amelia's living-room:

En el centro *hay un sofá de piel…*	In the centre there is a leather sofa…
… y una gran butaca **enfrente.**	… and a large sofa opposite.
Al fondo *hay una chimenea.*	At the far end there is a chimney.

Other expressions and prepositions that describe where something is include:

entre   (among, between):

> *Está* **entre** *la silla y la pared.*
>
> *La habitación de los invitados está* **entre** *el dormitorio y el estudio.*

sobre, en, encima (de)   (on, on top (of)):

> *Los papeles están* **sobre** *la mesa.*
>
> *El bolígrafo está* **en** *la mesa.*
>
> *Los papeles están* **encima de** *la cama.*

detrás (de)   (behind):

> *El niño está escondido* **detrás del** *árbol.*
>
> *La casa está* **detrás de** *la iglesia.*

delante (de)   (in front of, before):

> *Tengo el coche* **delante del** *supermercado.*
>
> *Las plantas están* **delante de** *la ventana.*

al lado (de)   (beside, next to):

> *La lámpara está* **al lado de** *la máquina de escribir.*
>
> *El cuadro está* **al lado de** *la estantería.*

dentro (de)   (inside, within):

> *Está* **dentro del** *armario.*
>
> *El espejo roto está* **dentro de** *la cómoda.*

a la izquierda   (on/to the left).

a la derecha   (on/to the right).

Actividad 5.9

Teresa gives Omar a description of her father's study in the house where she lived as a child. Look at the picture below and complete the gaps in her description with the appropriate prepositions from those in *Atando cabos*. In some cases more than one answer is possible. Use your viewpoint as the point of reference.

Teresa describe a Omar el despacho que su padre tenía cuando ella era pequeña. Mirando el dibujo, rellene los espacios con algunas de las preposiciones mencionadas.

El despacho del padre de Teresa

El despacho de mi padre era amplio y confortable. Tenía un escritorio, y ...... del escritorio, un sillón. ...... había dos sillas para las visitas. ...... había dos sillones, y ...... los sillones, una lámpara. ...... de la mesa tenía siempre muchos papeles y también una lámpara .... También había un teléfono .... A la izquierda del escritorio tenía una mesa y ...... ella, la máquina de escribir.

...... del despacho había una ventana, ... dos grandes estanterías con libros.

En el suelo, ... del escritorio, había una gran alfombra.

Curiosidad~

En España, la mayor parte de la gente vive en las ciudades, en bloques de pisos, que cuando son pequeños, se llaman apartamentos. En las afueras de la ciudad hay más casas, torres o chalés. En los últimos años se han puesto de moda las casas adosadas o semiadosadas. En el campo, las antiguas viviendas rurales, que en Andalucía se llaman 'cortijos', en Cataluña 'masías' y en el País Vasco 'caseríos', son cada vez más raras y muchos pueblos se han quedado casi desiertos por haber emigrado sus habitantes a las ciudades. Con todo, muchas personas vuelven a sus pueblos de origen y tienen una segunda casa en el campo o en la playa, donde pasan las vacaciones o los fines de semana.

chalé
a suburban house with
a garden

casas adosadas
in the style of British
terraced houses

Sección 3

In this *sección* you can hear people from Toledo talking about their homes. Some live in modern flats and some in older houses which, according to one of the owners, might just be haunted.

Key learning points

- Describing a house

- Writing a semi-formal letter for a language exchange

- Study skills: dictionary skills

Actividad 5.10

1 Before you listen to Extract 10 on the Interviews Cassette, make sure you know the meaning of the words below.

Antes de escuchar el Extracto 10 en la Cinta de entrevistas, asegúrese que conoce el significado de las siguientes palabras.

planta (la)	*floor*	('… la primera planta del edificio.')
casco (antiguo) (el)	*quarter, district*	('… el casco antiguo de la ciudad.')
antiguo	*old, antique*	('Es un mueble muy antiguo.')
portería (la)	*caretaker's lodge*	('Hoy en día hay pocas viviendas que tengan porterías.')
sótano (el)	*basement*	('Muchas casas antiguas tienen sótano.')
yeso (el)	*plaster*	('La casa es de yeso y piedra.')

azulejo (el)	*tile*	('Los azulejos de la cocina son blancos.')
sábana (la)	*sheet*	('Las sábanas son estampadas.')
(vivienda) unifamiliar	*(dwellings) for only one family*	('Vivo en una vivienda unifamiliar.')
portero automático (el)	*entry phone*	('En mi casa hay portero automático.')

2 Now listen to Extract 10 of the Interviews Cassette and tick to show whether the following statements about Maribel are true or false. Rewrite any incorrect statements.

Escuche el Extracto 10 en la Cinta de entrevistas e indique si las siguientes frases son verdaderas o falsas. Corrija la información falsa.

	Verdadero	Falso
(a) Vive en una casa unifamiliar.	❑	❑
(b) Es una casa pequeña, pero muy bonita.	❑	❑
(c) Tiene portería.	❑	❑
(d) Vive en un edificio de dos pisos.	❑	❑

Marcos, on the other hand, lives in a very special house.

Actividad 5.11

Listen to Extract 11 on the Interviews Cassette, in which Marcos describes his house, and tick to show whether the following statements are true or false.

Escuche el Extracto 11 en la Cinta de entrevistas e indique si las siguientes frases son verdaderas o falsas.

	Verdadero	Falso
1 Vive en una casa moderna.	❑	❑
2 Hay un patio en medio.	❑	❑
3 Tiene pocas ventanas.	❑	❑
4 Tiene muchas macetas con flores.	❑	❑
5 Tiene muchos adornos.	❑	❑

Actividad 5.12

1 Now that you've heard descriptions of two houses in Toledo, look at the questions over the page about your own home and prepare answers. Try not to take more than five minutes for your preparation.

Acaba de oír una descripción de dos casas en Toledo. Lea primero las preguntas sobre su propia casa y prepare las respuestas.

Ejemplo

¿Dónde vive, en una casa o en un piso?

Vivo en una casa.

(a) ¿Cuántas plantas tiene?

(b) ¿Está céntrica/o?

(c) ¿Cuántas habitaciones tiene?

(d) ¿Tiene patio, balcones o jardín?

(e) ¿Es exterior?

2 Use your answers to help you write a letter suggesting a house exchange. Don't forget to use expressions of location and place.

Escriba una descripción de su casa con vistas a hacer un intercambio de casas.

Start by saying:

'Me gustaría intercambiar mi casa con alguien en España con una casa similar durante el mes de X…'

and finish with:

'Si está interesado/a, escriba a…'

Actividad 5.13

1 Certain words can be confusing because they are spelt in the same way as others with different meanings. For example, there are different meanings for the word *planta*. Look at the list of definitions below, taken from a dictionary.

Mire las siguientes definiciones de la palabra 'planta' en el diccionario.

> **planta** *f* **1** (Bot) plant
> **planta de interior** houseplant, indoor plant
> **2** (Arquit) **(a)** (plano) plan **(b)** (piso) floor; **primera/tercera**
> ∼ second/fourth floor (AmE), first/third floor (BrE); **una**
> **casa de dos** ∼**s** a two-story house; **grandes ofertas**
> **en la** ∼ **de señoras** big savings in the ladies' fashion
> department
> **planta baja** first floor (AmE), ground floor (BrE)
> **3** (Tec) (instalación) plant
> **4** (del pie) sole
> **5** (tipo, apariencia): **de buena** ∼ fine-looking
> **6** (de empleados) staff

(*Concise Oxford Spanish Dictionary,* 1996, p. 488, Oxford University Press)

2 Now look up the words opposite, taken from the Audio Drama transcript. Write two sentences to illustrate the different meanings of each, as you find them in your dictionary.

Escriba dos frases con cada una de las palabras a continuación ilustrando diferentes significados de éstas.

Ejemplo

cuarto

El cuarto de baño está en la planta baja.   (a room)
Son las nueve y cuarto.   (a quarter)

(a) hoja

(b) casco

(c) piso

~ENTIENDO:DEBO ANUNCIAR A MI SEÑOR QUE EL SEÑOR ABOGADO DE LOS SEÑORES VECINOS DESEA VERLO.¿EL SEÑOR ABOGADO SABRÍA ANTICIPARME POR QUÉ ASUNTO ES,SI ES TAN AMABLE?

(*El País semanal,* 29 de diciembre de 1996)

Actividad 5.14

To end this unit, you will revise some vocabulary. Look at the sets of words below and underline the odd one out in each case.

Lea los siguientes grupos de palabras y subraye en cada grupo la palabra que no pertenezca al grupo.

1 almohada, cortina, persiana, sábanas, toallas

2 apartamento, piso, estudio, chalé, cuarto

3 mesa, ventana, puerta, pared, techo

4 dormitorio, despacho, lavabo, salón, cuadro

5 cómoda, mesa, comedor, sofá, estantería

Resumiendo...

Now you can:

- describe a flat or a house
- pronounce *ll, y* and *ñ*
- use the imperative (*tú* and *vosotros* forms)
- give commands
- give advice
- use prepositions of place
- write a semi-formal letter for a house exchange

Unidad 6
Al pan, pan y al vino, vino

This *unidad* focuses on food and drink. Omar and Teresa go to a bar to have a snack and discuss what happened at Doña Amelia's house. You will learn how routines and habits in Spain relating to eating and drinking vary from those in other countries. The pastrycook in a traditional cake shop in Toledo tells you about her work, and the Interviews Cassette takes you on a visit to the local market place.

Sección 1

Teresa and Omar are in a bar in Toledo. They order a few *tapas* and talk about Teresa's past relationships and their future together.

Key learning points

- Offering food and drinks
- Ordering and paying for food and drinks
- Talking about relationships
- Study skills: categorizing vocabulary

Actividad 6.1

1 Episode 6 of *El idioma del amor* takes place after Teresa and Omar have left Doña Amelia's. Before you listen to the cassette, try to predict what's going to happen. In each pair of sentences below, tick the one you think is true.

Antes de escuchar la cinta, prediga lo que va a suceder. Indique la frase que cree que es correcta de cada par.

(a) (i) Teresa y Omar están contentos. ❑

    (ii) Teresa y Omar están disgustados. ❑

(b) (i) Teresa y Omar regresan inmediatamente a Madrid. ❑

    (ii) Teresa y Omar se quedan un rato más en Toledo. ❑

(c) (i) Teresa no quiere hablar de la actitud de su madre. ❑

    (ii) Teresa explica a Omar la razón de la actitud de su madre. ❑

(d) (i) Teresa y Omar deciden continuar su relación en secreto. ❑

    (ii) Teresa y Omar deciden casarse. ❑

2 Now listen to Episode 6 on the Audio Drama cassette and find out whether you were right or not.

Ahora escuche el Episodio 6 del Radiodrama y averigüe si acertó en sus predicciones.

Actividad 6.2

Listen again to Episode 6 (from the beginning up to '*¿Sigues enfadada?*') and read the *Cabos sueltos* opposite. Then indicate which of the expressions are used by Teresa and Omar for offering and asking for drinks and snacks.

Escuche otra vez el episodio 6 del Radiodrama y lea el siguiente 'Cabos sueltos'. Identifique cuáles de las siguientes expresiones para ofrecer y pedir comidas y bebidas se usan.

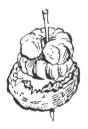

Pincho de huevo

Gambas al ajillo

Patatas bravas

Pincho de tortilla

Cabos sueltos

En el bar

Here are some useful expressions for offering, ordering and paying for drinks and snacks in Spain:

To attract attention:

> *¿Camarero/a, por favor?*
>
> *¡Oiga, por favor!*
>
> *¡Oye!* (informal)

To offer food or drinks to somebody:

> *¿Qué quiere(s) tomar?*
>
> *¿Qué quiere(s) comer?*
>
> *¿Qué va(s) a tomar?*

To order food and drinks:

> *Yo voy a tomar una ración de calamares.*
>
> *Para mí, un refresco de naranja y un pincho de tortilla.*
>
> *¿Me pone(s) una tapa de calamares y un agua mineral?*
>
> *Dos tintos y una cerveza, por favor.*

To pay:

> *¿Me trae(s) la cuenta, por favor?*
>
> *¿Me cobra(s)?*
>
> *¿Se cobra?*

Curiosidad~

Los pinchos y las tapas son muy populares en España. Consisten en pequeñas porciones de comida que se toman en los bares, generalmente antes de la comida del mediodía o por la tarde. Los hay de muchos tipos: patatas preparadas de diferentes formas, marisco, carne, huevos, ensaladas, etc.

El significado original de la palabra 'tapa' es 'cubierta', puesto que originalmente las tapas se servían cubriendo los vasos de vino, cerveza o cualquier otra bebida a la que acompañaban para evitar que cayesen moscas dentro. Los pinchos son muy similares a las 'tapas' y se llaman así porque se 'pinchan' con un palillo.

While they are eating their *tapas,* Teresa tells Omar why Doña Amelia is so prickly about her daughter's relationships with men.

Actividad 6.3

Listen to the next part of Episode 6 (from where Teresa says *'Un poco, pero estoy mejor'* to where Omar says *'Necesita tiempo'*) and put the following sentences in the order in which you hear them.

Escuche la segunda parte de la grabación y luego ordene las frases siguientes según las oiga.

1   La familia del padre de Carmen se marchó al extranjero.

2   Teresa se quedó embarazada.

3   La familia del padre de Carmen dio algo de dinero.

4   Doña Amelia se quedó viuda.

5   El padre de Carmen tenía miedo.

6   Fue una noche tonta, una equivocación.

Actividad 6.4

1   As you can hear, Teresa and Omar are talking about relationships. Study the following list of words and phrases used to talk about relationships: note which of them appear in the dialogue and to whom they refer.

Lea la siguiente lista de expresiones para hablar de relaciones amorosas: identifique cuáles de ellas se mencionan en el diálogo y a quién se refieren.

> salir juntos, boda, querer a alguien, enamorarse,
> casarse, quedarse viuda, dejar a alguien, (tener) relaciones,
> quedarse embarazada, engañar a alguien

2   Now, using the Transcript Booklet, write down the form and context in which the expressions listed in *Cabos sueltos* appear.

Vaya a la transcripción y escriba en qué contexto aparecen las palabras y expresiones.

Ejemplo

Expresión	Uso	Con referencia a...
querer a alguien	¿Pero no te quería?	Teresa's former boyfriend (Carmen's father)

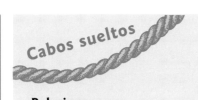

Cabos sueltos

Relaciones

Frequently used expressions referring to relationships include:

estar enamorado, -a	to be in love
salir juntos	to go out together
ser novios	to be going out together (more formally)
estar prometidos	to be engaged
casarse por la iglesia	to get married in church
casarse por el juzgado	to get married in a registry office
ser pareja de hecho	common law couple
vivir juntos	to live together
separarse de alguien	to separate from someone
divorciarse de alguien	to divorce someone
quedarse viudo / viuda	to be widowed / left a widower / widow
engañar a alguien	to cheat (on) someone
dejar a alguien	to leave someone

Actividad 6.5

Now divide the expressions in the *Cabos sueltos* box into two lists: those which might be appropriate to an older generation (*los abuelos*), the other to a younger one.

Categorizing vocabulary

Putting vocabulary into categories is a good way of helping to memorize it. You will get even more out of this process if you decide which groups are likely to be most useful for you. When you make lists of this kind, try picking out and highlighting those expressions you are fairly sure you are going to use.

Sección 2

Now is your chance to find out more about Spanish eating habits and daily routines. You will also compare Spanish lifestyles and customs with those elsewhere in Europe.

Key learning points

- Talking about routine and using reflexive verbs

- Pronouncing *r* and *rr*

- Study skills: scanning a text

In recent times, sandwich bars or cafés have become very fashionable. In Spain, most sandwiches are made with *pan de barra* (French sticks) and are called *bocadillos* or, more informally, *bocatas*. A selection of the best *bocadillos* from various bars is shown below.

Actividad 6.6

1 Read the text next to the illustrations below and make a list of the ingredients in the sandwiches and their side dishes.

Lea el texto y haga una lista de los ingredientes de los bocadillos y sandwiches.

Vegetal

**Bocadillo verde con ensalada y refresco: 1.250 pesetas.
(Todo Sandwich)**

Serrano

**Mini de jamón con tomate, con refresco y café. Cuesta 500 pesetas.
(De La Garriga)**

Clásico

**Calamares con pan recién hecho. Con ensalada y bebida, 595 pesetas.
(Míster Bocata)**

Campero

**Lomo y pimientos verdes. El menú lo completan patatas, refresco y postre. Por 625 pesetas.
(Bocata World)**

Malagueño

Cangrejo, jamón de York, lechuga y salsa rosa. Con ensalada y caña, 890 pesetas. (De Bocata y Olé)

Mexicano

Lleva carne con salsa picante. Acompañado de ensalada, refresco y helado: 1.250 pesetas. (De Taruffi)

(Roig, AM, extracto de *Bocadillos en alza*, El País semanal, no. 210, 1995)

2   Now write a sentence saying which sandwich you like and why.

Ahora escriba qué bocadillo le gusta más y por qué.

Ejemplo

Mi bocadillo favorito es el 'serrano' porque *me gusta el jamón.*

Mi bocadillo favorito es el 'clásico' porque *me gustan los calamares*.

Atando cabos

Verbos pronominales

In the previous *sección* you learned vocabulary and expressions for talking about relationships. Some of the verbs were rather different from the ones you have seen before, in that they add an object pronoun at the end of the infinitive. These are called 'pronominal verbs'. Examples are: *casarse, separarse, enamorarse, divorciarse*.

Pronominal verbs are accompanied by an object pronoun that agrees in number and gender with the subject of the verb:

Me <u>caso</u> con Omar.	I am marrying Omar. (**I** <u>am marrying</u> **myself** with Omar.)
*¿Tú piensas que no **nos** <u>conoc**emos**</u> suficientemente?*	Do you think **we** don't <u>know</u> **each other** well enough?

This type of verb can have many different meanings. One of the most common is the 'reflexive' meaning where the action of the verb is performed by the subject upon him/herself, as in:

*Teresa se <u>levant**a**</u> muy pronto.*	Teresa <u>gets</u> **(herself)** <u>up</u> very early.

You may be familiar with other reflexive verbs such as those used to talk about routines, for example: *ducharse, lavarse, peinarse, vestirse.*

The full list of object pronouns used with pronominal verbs is: *me, te, se, nos, os, se.*

This is how these verbs are conjugated:

(yo)	**me**	levanto
(tú)	**te**	levantas
(él/ella/usted)	**se**	levanta
(nosotros, -as)	**nos**	levantamos
(vosotros, -as)	**os**	levantáis
(ellos/ellas/ustedes)	**se**	levantan

You will notice that the verb endings are no different from those used when the verb has no attached pronoun. The object pronoun goes **in front of** the verb, as in:

*Normalmente, **me** levant**o** a las ocho de la mañana.*

However, when the verb is in the infinitive, imperative or gerund form, the pronoun **follows** the verb and is attached to it.

To look up a pronominal verb in the dictionary, you need to search for the infinitive with the **third person** pronoun attached, e.g.: *levantarse* (= to get (oneself) up).

Now you are going to practise using pronominal verbs to talk about daily routines. You will hear about a typical day in the lives of Teresa and Omar, before talking about a typical day in your own life.

Actividad 6.7

1 Listen to Teresa's daily routine in Extract 17 (part one) on the Activities Cassette and note down which pronominal verbs are used.

   Escuche la rutina de Omar y Teresa en la Cinta de actividades y anote los verbos pronominales que aparecen.

2 Listen to Teresa's routine in Extract 17 (part two) and change the sentences to the third person singular.

   Escuche la rutina de Teresa y cambie las frases a la tercera persona del singular.

3 Listen to Omar's daily routine in Extract 18 (part one) of the Activities Cassette and note down in Spanish two things that Omar does and Teresa does not do.

Escuche la rutina de Omar y anote en español dos cosas que hace él que no hace Teresa.

4 Listen to Omar's daily routine in Extract 18 (part two) and translate the English sentences about his routine into Spanish.

Escuche la rutina de Omar y traduzca las frases inglesas sobre su rutina al español.

Actividad 6.8

Now go to Extract 19 on the Activities Cassette and answer the questions about your routine.

Ahora escuche el Extracto 19 en la Cinta de actividades y responda a las preguntas sobre su rutina.

Curiosidad~

El horario comercial español es, por lo general, diferente del de muchos otros países. Las tiendas normalmente abren a las nueve de la mañana y cierran a la una y media o dos del mediodía. Por la tarde, abren a las cuatro y media o cinco y cierran a las ocho. Los grandes almacenes y los hipermercados no suelen cerrar al mediodía. En algunas zonas turísticas, las tiendas están abiertas por la noche hasta muy tarde.

El horario escolar es también distinto. Las clases empiezan a las ocho y media o nueve de la mañana y acaban a la una o una y media del mediodía. Después hay una pausa para la comida (que generalmente se hace en casa) y los niños vuelven al colegio de tres o tres y media a cinco o cinco y media de la tarde.

Por las tardes, muchos niños van a clases de música, gimnasia, ballet, artes marciales y otras disciplinas. Muchos aprenden idiomas y algunos van a clases particulares, si necesitan ayuda con sus estudios.

While links between European countries have been growing stronger in the recent past, each nation has retained much of its own individuality. Routines, habits and customs vary from one country to another. The article overleaf illustrates this.

Actividad 6.9

Read the article and answer the following questions in Spanish.

Lea el texto y responda a las siguientes preguntas en español.

LOS EUROPEOS

EL DEPORTE

60 millones de europeos son socios de algún grupo deportivo. El fútbol es el más practicado, seguido del tenis y la natación.

VICIOS Y COSTUMBRES

Griegos, portugueses e irlandeses invierten en comer, beber y fumar el doble que el resto de los europeos. Los italianos consumen más trigo, los irlandeses más patatas, los griegos más verdura, los franceses más carne y los finlandeses más productos lácteos. Los españoles tienen una de las dietas más equilibradas.

ASÍ NOS ENTRETENEMOS

Los europeos pasan tres horas al día pendientes del televisor. En la UE hay 40 aparatos de televisión por cada cien habitantes y casi el doble de radios, pero en España hay más televisores que receptores radiofónicos.

BODAS Y BAUTIZOS

La Europa de los Quince ha aumentado un 30% su territorio con la incorporación de Austria, Finlandia y Suecia. El país comunitario más grande es Francia y el más pequeño, Luxemburgo.

En 1992 nacieron más de cuatro millones de europeos y murieron tres millones y medio (la población total ascendía a 370 millones, incluyendo Austria, Finlandia y Suecia). Se celebraron dos millones de bodas y uno de cada tres matrimonios acabó en divorcio. Los portugueses son los más aficionados a casarse y los ingleses a divorciarse.

(Adaptado de un artículo aparecido en *El País semanal*, no. 228, domingo 2 de julio de 1995)

1   ¿Cuál es el deporte más popular en Europa?

2   ¿En qué países se come, fuma y bebe más?

3   ¿Qué país tiene una de las mejores dietas?

4   ¿Qué medio de comunicación es más popular en España?

5   ¿En qué país europeo hay más divorcios?

Scanning a text

Scanning texts is a useful reading strategy. First of all, you have to be clear about what information you want to discover. That is why it helps to read activity questions carefully and understand them before you start reading the text. Then you can concentrate on finding the right answers.

Pronunciación: 'r' y 'rr'

r is trilled (strong) at the beginning of a word (*ruido, ratón, respuesta*) and after *l*, *n* or *s*, as in:

   alrededor, Enrique, Israel.

It becomes a flapped (soft) *r* when it appears in any other position, as in:

   mirada, calor, parada.

rr is always pronounced as a trilled *r*. It only appears between vowels (*perro, carretera, socorro*).

Actividad 6.10

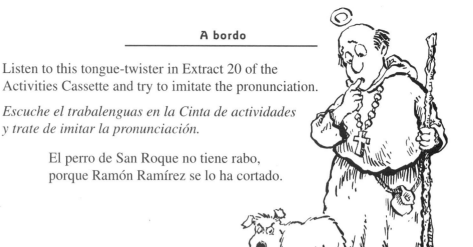

Listen to this tongue-twister in Extract 20 of the
Activities Cassette and try to imitate the pronunciation.

*Escuche el trabalenguas en la Cinta de actividades
y trate de imitar la pronunciación.*

> El perro de San Roque no tiene rabo,
> porque Ramón Ramírez se lo ha cortado.

San Roque y su perro

Sección 3

Now let's take a look at food in Spain. The country is famous for its fruit and
vegetables, and Spaniards have a love of food which is reflected in the variety
of the regional cuisine.

> **Key learning points**
> - Using the impersonal *se*
> - Explaining how to cook a recipe
> - Using vocabulary relating to food
> - Study skills: defining words

Actividad 6.11

1 How much do you know about Spanish eating habits? Tick to show
   whether you think these sentences are true or false.

   *¿Conoce bien los hábitos alimentarios españoles? Indique si cree que las
   frases siguientes son verdaderas o falsas.*

	Verdadero	Falso
En España...		
(a) ... la comida principal es la del mediodía.	❏	❏
(b) ... el desayuno no es muy importante.	❏	❏
(c) ... la comida es un acto social.	❏	❏
(d) ... no es normal comer en familia.	❏	❏
(e) ... los niños generalmente cenan a media tarde.	❏	❏

2 Now listen to Extract 12 on the Interviews Cassette and check whether you were right.

Ahora escuche el Extracto 12 de la Cinta de entrevistas y compruebe si sus respuestas son correctas.

Actividad 6.12

It is often helpful to associate related words, such as *trabajo* (noun) and *trabajar* (verb). Complete the chart below by adding the verb or noun to whichever word is listed.

Complete el siguiente recuadro.

Sustantivo	Verbo	Verbo	Sustantivo
cena		comer	
merienda		desayunar	
bebida		almorzar	

Curiosidad ~

En España hay tres comidas al día:

El desayuno es la primera comida del día y no suele ser muy abundante: café con tostadas o galletas, a veces acompañado de un zumo de fruta.

La comida del mediodía es la principal. Normalmente la gente come en casa, entre la una y media y las tres de la tarde. Suele consistir en tres platos (primer plato, segundo plato y postre) y a menudo va seguida de café.

La cena es la última comida del día y no es tan abundante como la del mediodía. Por lo general, en España la gente cena sobre las diez de la noche.

Es bastante común comer algo entre el desayuno y la comida (como, por ejemplo, un bocadillo o algún dulce) y entre la comida y la cena (la merienda, que puede ser un bocadillo, o café con pasteles o galletas, o fruta).

Actividad 6.13

Imagine you wanted to help someone cook a typically Spanish dish.

1 The recipe opposite gives the different stages in making a Spanish omelette, but unfortunately they are not in the right order. Put the steps in the right order. (The first one has been done for you.)

Aquí tiene los pasos para la preparación de una tortilla española. Ordénelos.

TORTILLA DE PATATAS

Ingredientes: 2 patatas grandes   4 huevos
                1 cebolla mediana   sal   aceite

Pasos

...	Freír las patatas y la cebolla.
...	Añadir las patatas y la cebolla a los huevos batidos.
...	Hacer por el otro lado la tortilla.
1	Pelar y lavar las patatas.
...	Echar sal al gusto.
...	Cortar las patatas y la cebolla en trozos pequeños.
...	Echar todo a la sartén y freír.
...	Batir los huevos.
...	Llenar la sartén de aceite hasta la mitad y calentar.
...	Dar la vuelta con un plato o tapadera.
...	Quitar el aceite sobrante de la sartén.
...	Pelar la cebolla.

Atando cabos

Descripción de un proceso usando 'se'

Se can be used with a verb in the third person (for example, *come* or *comen*, from *comer*) to indicate a process. The verb agrees with the item that undergoes the process, as in:

> **Se pela** *la fruta.*   The fruit is peeled.
>
> **Se cortan** *las manzanas.*   The apples are cut / diced.

As you have already seen, *se* is also the third person pronoun used with pronominal verbs:

> *Carmen* **se** *ducha todos los días.*
>
> *Omar y Teresa* **se** *levantan temprano.*

But compare:

> **Se** *echa el huevo en la sartén.*

These two structures are virtually identical in form, but the difference in meaning must not be confused.

The main difference is that, with pronominal verbs, the full range of pronouns (*me, te, se, nos, os*) can be used, depending on the various subjects (*yo, tú, él, ella, usted, nosotros, (-as), vosotros, (-as), ellos, ellas, ustedes*) whereas for describing processes, only *se* can be used.

If an object pronoun is also needed in the sentence, it will be placed between the *se* and the verb:

> *Se* **le** *añaden los huevos.*   The eggs are added **to it**.

2 Now rewrite the recipe, using *se* plus the appropriate form of each verb. The box below contains some phrases for linking time or sequence, to help you make your explanation clearer. Make use of all of them in order to divide the instructions into different stages.

Ahora vuelva a escribir la receta usando la estructura impersonal y las siguientes palabras.

primero	luego	después
cuando (estén listas)	entonces	finalmente

In the Interviews Cassette, Inés Gárate, a pastry cook from a famous *pastelería* in Toledo, explains the history behind marzipan-making. Marzipan has always been very popular since it is made from local products, and also because it was not forbidden by any religion. This was an important factor, since from the eleventh century and throughout the Middle Ages, Christians, Jews and Moslems lived together in the city.

Ingredientes para el mazapán: almendra, azúcar, huevos y miel

Actividad 6.14

Inés also describes how to make marzipan, using the impersonal expressions.

Listen to Extract 13 on the Interviews Cassette and fill the gaps in the following brief description of the marzipan-making process by putting the verbs in brackets into the correct impersonal form.

Escuche el Extracto 13 y complete esta breve descripción del proceso de fabricación del mazapán.

Primero, (lavar) ...... la almendra. Después (mezclar) ...... la almendra con los azúcares. (Moler) ...... la masa, (triturar) ......, (dar) ...... dos pasadas y luego... le (ir) ...... dando diferentes formas y... le (ir) ...... dando distintos rellenos.

Curiosidad~

La cocina española no sólo ha tomado tradiciones y costumbres de los árabes, sino también ha tomado productos de Hispanoamérica, como la patata, el chocolate, la vainilla, el cacahuete, el maíz y el tomate.

Actividad 6.15

1 Read the descriptions of fruits and vegetables on the left and match them with the appropriate name on the right.

Lea las descripciones de frutas y verduras de la columna de la izquierda y enlácelas con la palabra apropiada de la columna de la derecha.

(a) un cítrico redondo y anaranjado

(b) una verdura larga y anaranjada

(c) una fruta roja, amarilla o verde por fuera y blanca por dentro

(d) una verdura de hojas verdes y blancas que se usa en ensaladas

(e) una fruta larga y amarilla

(f) una verdura redondeada con el centro blando, recubierta de pequeñas hojas verdes

(g) una fruta tropical, amarilla por dentro y marrón por fuera

(h) parecen paraguas

(i) una hortaliza marrón por fuera y blanca por dentro

(j) es roja por fuera y por dentro y se come con ensaladas y con espaguettis

(k) tiene capas concéntricas por dentro y hace llorar

(l) una hortaliza larga, verde por fuera y blanca por dentro

(i) patatas

(ii) pepino

(iii) lechuga

(iv) cebolla

(v) naranja

(vi) champiñones

(vii) zanahoria

(viii) tomate

(ix) plátano

(x) manzana

(xi) piña

(xii) alcachofa

Cabos sueltos

Notice the different phrases listed below. They might be useful for describing (or asking for) items of food whose names you might not know. For example:

Tiene capas concéntricas. *(cebolla)*

Se come con ensaladas. *(tomate)*

Se usa en ensaladas. *(lechuga, cebolla, aceitunas, etc.)*

Parecen paraguas. *(champiñones)*

Es verde **por fuera** y blanca **por dentro.** *(alcachofa, pepino)*

2 Here are some less common items. How would you describe them if you wanted to ask for them at a Spanish market?

Piense cómo describiría los siguientes alimentos si quisiera comprarlos en un mercado español.

(a) rhubarb

(b) fennel

(c) celery

Defining words

You've just found out how to describe different types of food in terms of shape, colour, what they look like and how they are used. You may well find that you do not know, or are unable to remember, certain words in Spanish, so it is very useful to be able to describe something. People will then understand what you mean and will probably also give you the word you need.

Curiosidad~

Adivinanza

Blancos son,

las gallinas los ponen,

con manteca se fríen,

y con pan se comen.

¿Puede adivinar qué son? *

Actividad 6.16

Listen to Extract 14 on the Interviews Cassette and answer the following questions.

Escuche el Extracto 14 en la Cinta de entrevistas y responda a las siguientes preguntas.

1 ¿Dónde ocurre este diálogo?

2 Identifique las cinco hortalizas que compran las señoras.

3 ¿Cuánto cuesta cada cosa?

4 ¿Qué piensa la señora del precio de las alcachofas?

* *¡Huevos!*

124

Actividad 6.17

Will you be shopping for food soon? Look at this list of food from a supermarket and tick those items you would like to have delivered to your home. This should help you retain the vocabulary that you have learned and perhaps pick up some new words.

Haga su lista de la compra en español. Marque los ingredientes que necesita.

Verduras y hortalizas		**Frutas**		**Condimentos**	
judías verdes	❏	naranjas	❏	mostaza	❏
guisantes	❏	peras	❏	mahonesa	❏
tomates	❏	manzanas	❏	aceite	❏
patatas	❏	melón	❏	vinagre	❏
cebollas	❏	melocotones	❏	sal	❏
pimientos	❏	higos	❏	**Dulces**	
ajo	❏	uvas	❏	galletas	❏
calabacín	❏	nectarinas	❏	magdalenas	❏
berenjena	❏	**Legumbres**		mermelada	❏
col	❏	habas	❏	chocolate	❏
lechuga	❏	judías	❏	miel	❏
apio	❏	garbanzos	❏	**Productos lácteos**	
nabo	❏	guisantes	❏	**y huevos**	
brécol	❏	lentejas	❏	huevos	❏
hinojo	❏	**Pescados**		queso	❏
Carnes		merluza	❏	yogur	❏
vaca	❏	bacalao	❏	leche	❏
cerdo	❏	trucha	❏	mantequilla	❏
cordero	❏	calamar	❏	margarina	❏
pollo	❏	**Bebidas**		**Cereales**	
Fiambres		agua mineral	❏	harina blanca	❏
jamón de York	❏	zumo	❏	harina integral	❏
jamón serrano	❏	vino tinto	❏	arroz blanco	❏
chorizo	❏	vino blanco	❏	arroz integral	❏
salmón ahumado	❏			maíz	❏

Resumiendo ...

Now you can:

- offer food and drinks
- order and pay for food and drinks
- talk about daily routines
- talk about relationships
- pronounce *r* and *rr*
- explain how to cook a recipe
- use vocabulary relating to food

Unidad 7 *El mercadillo*

To make their dreams come true, Omar and Teresa go shopping for a very special item, after which something unexpected happens. They make a list of things they need for their honeymoon. When she gets home, Teresa finds her answering machine full of messages about shopping.

In Toledo, you will visit the local market, where someone is buying traditional pottery.

Sección 1

In this *sección* you will listen to Episode 7 of the Audio Drama, in which Teresa and Omar go shopping. In the evening, Teresa decides to pick Omar up from his place of work when he finishes his shift.

Key learning points

- Asking for and giving opinions
- Revising asking questions
- Using vocabulary and expressions for shopping
- Study skills: listening for clues in intonation

Actividad 7.1

1 Match the words on the left with their translations on the right.

Una las palabras de la izquierda con su traducción de la derecha.

caro	*cheap*
barato	*sales*
cambio	*size*
rebajas	*expensive*
talla	*change*
probar	*to bargain*
escaparate	*shop window*
pagar a plazos	*to try on*
recibo	*to pay in instalments*
regatear	*receipt*

2 Listen to Episode 7 of the Audio Drama, from the beginning to '*Este tipo de vestido vale este precio*', and answer the following questions.

Escuche el Episodio 7 del Radiodrama desde el principio hasta 'Este tipo de vestido vale este precio' y conteste las siguientes preguntas.

(a) ¿En qué tienda están?

(b) ¿Qué quieren comprar?

(c) ¿Cuántas prendas se prueba Teresa?

(d) ¿Qué color escogen finalmente?

(e) ¿Cuánto vale la prenda que compran?

De compras

In the first part of the Audio Drama you heard several phrases involving the words *probar*, *talla* and *costar*, such as:

> **Me** lo voy a **probar**.
>
> Voy a **probarme** el otro.
>
> ¡Y es justo mi **talla**!
>
> ¿Cuánto **cuesta**?

*Remember that clothes sizes in continental Europe are different from those used in the UK and US.

Here are some questions you might use or hear when shopping:

¿Qué talla usa?	What is your size?
¿Tiene una talla más grande?	Do you have (it in) a larger size?
¿Qué número de zapatos tiene?	What size shoes* do you take?
¿Tiene estos zapatos en el 38?	Have you got these shoes in size 38*?
¿Cuánto cuestan estos pantalones?	How much are these trousers?
¿Puedo probarme este vestido?	Can I try this dress on?

Actividad 7.2

Write a question using each of the following: *talla, costar, probarse.*

Escriba una pregunta con cada una de las siguientes palabras: talla, costar, probarse.

Ejemplo

¿Puedo probarme la falda?

Actividad 7.3

1   Listen to Episode 7 from where the narrator says '*Teresa toma los dos vestidos...*' to '*Este tipo de vestido vale este precio.*' What five opinions does Omar express about the dresses?

Escuche esta parte del Episodio 7 y tome nota de las cinco opiniones que da Omar.

Cabos sueltos

¿Qué te parece?

Here are ways of asking someone's opinion:

¿Qué tal?	How is it? / What does it look like?
¿Crees que me sienta bien?	Do you think it suits me?
¿Qué te parece?	What do you think?

Here are some typical replies:

Es *bonito / feo / elegante / original.*	It's nice / ugly / elegant / original.

Está pasado de moda.	It's out of fashion / old-fashioned.
Creo que es un poco caro.	I think it's a bit expensive.
Me gusta(n).	I like it / them.
No es mi estilo.	It's not my style. / It's not 'me'.

You can also add some adverbs to make your statement more precise:

Es un **poco** chillón.	It's a bit loud / jazzy / startling.
Son **demasiado** clásicos.	They are too classic / traditional.
Este modelo es **bastante** deportivo.	This model is quite sporty.

2   Write down what you think about the following selection of shoes.

Escriba qué le parece la siguiente selección de zapatos.

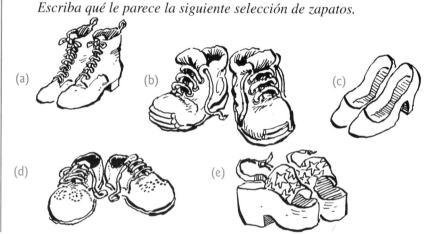

(a)   (b)   (c)   (d)   (e)

Actividad 7.4

1   Teresa is going to pick Omar up after work. What do you think will happen next? Choose one of the following options. Do not look at the *Clave* yet.

¿Qué cree que va a pasar?

(a) Teresa llega al restaurante y Omar no está allí.   ❏

(b) Teresa recibe una llamada en su teléfono móvil.   ❏

(c) Teresa ve desde el coche a su madre caminando por la calle.   ❏

(d) Teresa decide no ir a recoger a Omar y vuelve a su casa.   ❏

2   Listen to the second half of the Audio Drama episode, from *'Al final, Teresa sale de los almacenes contenta con su compra'* to the end, and check your answers.

Escuche el resto del episodio y compruebe su respuesta.

The drama of the situation is reflected in the voices of the two characters. This is shown in their intonation and the pitch of their voices.

Actividad 7.5

Listen to the second half of the episode again and match the short quotations listed below to the attitudes they reveal.

Escuche otra vez la segunda parte del episodio y una los siguientes extractos con las actitudes que reflejan.

¿Para tu boda?	(reconciliation)
¿Ah sí?	(fear / anxiety)
¿Sigues enfadada?	(surprise)
¡Mamá, estoy harta de que te metas en mi vida!	(warning)
¡No hagas esa locura, Teresa!	(anger)
¡Teresa! ¿Qué pasa?	(interest)

Listening for clues in intonation

When listening to spoken Spanish you should make use of all the clues you can pick up. The intonation and pitch can often help you understand the meaning.

Sección 2

While there are many *hipermercados* (large supermarkets or hypermarkets) and *centros comerciales* (shopping malls) in Spain nowadays, small specialist shops are still very common wherever you go.

Key learning points

- Using numbers and counting up to 2,000
- Revising direct object pronouns
- Using an answering machine
- Pronouncing *b* and *v*

Before you venture on a shopping trip, you will need to know what each Spanish shop sells. This will make your shopping easier!

Actividad 7.6

What can you buy in each of the shops in the drawing below? List appropriate items from the box against each shop name in the table.

Escriba los nombres de los artículos que puede comprar en cada tienda en el recuadro correspondiente.

hilo de coser, revistas, tabaco, longaniza, tiritas, sellos, periódicos, botones, clavos, jarabe, destornillador, chuletas

Ferretería	
Mercería	
Farmacia	
Librería	
Estanco	
Carnicería	

Actividad 7.7

Teresa and Omar are planning their honeymoon and thinking about the shopping they will need to do. They have not yet agreed where to go. Omar is assuming they are going to go somewhere cold, while Teresa would prefer somewhere warm.

Draw up shopping lists for each of them, using words from the box opposite.

Haga dos listas de compra con los siguientes objetos, teniendo en cuenta las preferencias de viaje de Teresa y Omar.

> una bufanda, unos guantes de cuero, un bañador, unas gafas
> de sol, un jersey, un sombrero de paja, unos pantalones de
> pana, unas sandalias, un gorro de lana, una camiseta de
> algodón, unos pantalones cortos, un parasol, unos calcetines
> de algodón, crema solar, unas botas, una minifalda

** In Spanish
America, *en
efectivo* is preferred
to *en metálico* when
talking about cash.*

When you go shopping, you will need *dinero*, which can be *en metálico* (or *en efectivo**); a *tarjeta de crédito*; or alternatively a *talón*, also called a *cheque*. You will also need to be able to use numbers effectively. In this *actividad*, you will deal with numbers under 2,000. But first, read *Atando cabos*.

Atando cabos

Números

0	*cero*	31	*treinta y un(o), -a*
1	*un(o), -a*	32	*treinta y dos*
2	*dos*	40	*cuarenta*
3	*tres*	50	*cincuenta*
4	*cuatro*	60	*sesenta*
5	*cinco*	70	*setenta*
6	*seis*	80	*ochenta*
7	*siete*	90	*noventa*
8	*ocho*	100	*cien / ciento -a*
9	*nueve*	101	*ciento un(o), -a*
10	*diez*	182	*ciento ochenta y dos*
11	*once*	200	*doscientos, -as*
12	*doce*	300	*trescientos, -as*
13	*trece*	400	*cuatrocientos, -as*
14	*catorce*	500	*quinientos, -as*
15	*quince*	600	*seiscientos, -as*
16	*dieciséis*	700	*setecientos, -as*
17	*diecisiete*	800	*ochocientos, -as*
18	*dieciocho*	900	*novecientos, -as*
19	*diecinueve*	1.000	*mil*
20	*veinte*	1.002	*mil dos*
21	*veintiún(o), -a*	1.999	*mil novecientos noventa y nueve*
22	*veintidós*	2.000	*dos mil*
30	*treinta*	3.000	*tres mil*

- The number *uno*, whether standing alone or as the ending of a larger number, drops the *o* before a masculine noun and becomes *una* before a feminine one:

  un peso, un dólar, veintiún dólares;

  una peseta, una libra esterlina, treinta y una libras esterlinas.

- Numbers between *dos* and *ciento noventa y nueve* have the same form in the masculine and the feminine (except for numbers ending with *un/una* such as *veintiún/uno/una, treinta y un/uno/una*).

- From 200 onwards, the hundreds have both masculine and feminine forms:

  doscientos francos, trescientas liras,

  doscientas pesetas, doscientas treinta y una pesetas.

- **Cien** is 100 (a hundred) when you are counting exactly or indicating a quantity of approximately one hundred:

  cien billetes, cien años.

- **Ciento** is used when followed by a further number (as in 'a hundred and… something'):

  ciento dos, ciento treinta y siete.

  (Note that there is no *y* after hundreds.)

- **Mil** does not change for the plural when describing multiple thousands:

  tres mil, cien mil.

  However, 'thousands of…' becomes '*miles de…*'

- Spanish uses the following system for large numbers and decimals:

  in large written numbers a full stop is used to separate thousands (*7.900*);

  the comma is used as a decimal point (*7,5*): this is pronounced '*siete coma cinco*'.

Actividad 7.8

Teresa and Omar have returned home from shopping and are checking their receipts. Write down how much the items cost and read aloud each answer as a sentence, giving the item and the amount.

Escriba cuánto valen estos objetos y lea en voz alta cada respuesta con la cantidad.

Ejemplo

(gorro: 2.500 ptas)

El gorro vale dos mil quinientas pesetas.

Actividad 7.9

You saw in previous *unidades* that there are personal pronouns for the subject of a verb as well as those used for the object. (Subject pronouns are less used than the English equivalents because in Spanish the subject is often understood from the form of the verb.) Fill in the following grid with the appropriate pronouns.

Complete el siguiente recuadro con los pronombres apropiados.

Personal (subject) pronouns	Personal (direct object) pronouns
yo	me
	te
él/ella/Ud.	
	nos
vosotros	
ellos/ellas/Uds.	

Atando cabos

Pronombres personales (objecto directo)

Look at these examples of the position and use of pronouns when they are direct objects:

1 Object pronouns usually come before the verb:

> Compraré **los vestidos** a final de mes.   **Los** compraré a final de mes.

> No encuentro **la tarjeta de crédito**.   No **la** encuentro.

2 However, object pronouns are always tagged onto the verb when it is in the affirmative imperative:

> Paga **la cuenta** en efectivo.   Pága**la** en efectivo.

3 When the infinitive or the gerund forms are used, object pronouns can either tag onto these forms or precede the conjugated verb:

> Deseo vender **el coche**.   Deseo vender**lo**.   **Lo** deseo vender.

> Estoy buscando **la bolsa**.   Estoy buscándo**la**.   **La** estoy buscando.

Activity 7.10

1 Listen to the Activities Cassette, Extract 21 (part one), in which somebody goes to a clothes shop. Pay attention to the use of the direct object pronouns.

Escuche el Extracto 21 (primera parte) en la Cinta de actividades, donde alguien va a una tienda de ropa. Fíjese en el uso de los pronombres.

2 Listen to the dialogue between a shop assistant and a customer in the Activities Cassette, Extract 21 (part two). Transform the sentences using the appropriate object pronouns.

Escuche el diálogo en la Cinta de actividades y transforme las frases usando los pronombres apropiados.

Ejemplo

You hear:

> *¿Tienen **camisas** de manga corta?*

You say:

> *¿**Las** tienen de manga corta?*

Pronunciación: 'b' y 'v'

The letters *b* and *v* are pronounced in Spanish in the same way. This sound is less explosive than the English 'b' and is therefore softer. Practise saying:

corbata   calabacín   tobillo   probar   llave   lavabo
vivir   nueve

However, in an initial position or after *m* or *n*, the sound is similar to the English 'b'. Practise saying:

combinación   bufanda   viva   cambio

Actividad 7.11

Now listen to some words containing this sound on Extract 22 of the Activities Cassette, and repeat them aloud in the gaps.

Escuche las palabras en la Cinta de actividades y repítalas en los espacios.

Sometimes it is not necessary to leave the house to go shopping: you can do it by phone (*ventas por teléfono*). On other occasions a friend might phone and ask you to go shopping. Teresa's answering machine is full of messages about some aspect of shopping. Here are some phrases that might help you when using an answering machine.

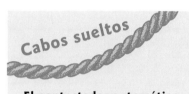

El contestador automático

Outgoing messages:

> *Hola, lo siento, no hay nadie en casa. Deja el mensaje después de la señal.*

> *Éste es el contestador automático de Maribel Segura. Si quieren dejar un mensaje, hablen después de la señal.*

To leave a message:

> *¡Hola! / ¡Buenos días! / ¡Buenas tardes!*

Le/te llamo para…	I'm phoning because…
Soy yo.	It's me.
Éste es un mensaje para…	This is a message for…
Volveré a llamar.	I'll phone again.

Actividad 7.12

1 Listen to Extract 23 (part one) on the Activities Cassette, which is about messages left on Teresa's answering machine, and make notes about them. (You will need the third person of the future tense of *volver: volverá*.)

Tome nota de los mensajes para Teresa en su contestador automático.

2 Listen to Extract 23 (part two) on the Activities Cassette and leave a message on the answerphone. Say who you are, that you will phone later, and then say goodbye.

Escuche la cinta y deje un mensaje en el contestador automático diciendo quién es usted, que llamará más tarde, y luego despídase.

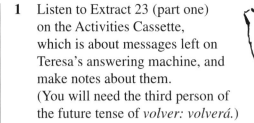

Sección 3

In this *sección* you will visit an open market (*un mercadillo*) in Toledo. These are very common in Spain and the huge range of items on sale promises an interesting morning out for anyone.

Key learning points

- Using demonstratives: *este, -ta / ese, -sa / aquel, -lla*

- Revising comparatives

- Study skills: vocabulary – building on words you know

Curiosidad~

En España, como en casi todos los países de clima templado, existe la costumbre de vender en la calle, en lo que se conoce como 'mercadillos', donde uno puede encontrar desde piezas de motor, libros de segunda mano, hasta muebles. Los mercadillos más conocidos y populares son los de Madrid ('El Rastro'), Barcelona ('Los Encantes') y Sevilla ('La Alameda'), pero en casi cada ciudad o pueblo se celebra regularmente un mercadillo.

Actividad 7.13

Write three different paragraphs describing a *mercado*, a *mercadillo* and a *supermercado*. The sentences below will help you.

Escriba tres párrafos que describan un mercado, un mercadillo y un supermercado.

> Es una gran extensión cubierta.
>
> En él venden marcas comerciales conocidas.
>
> Es un puesto de venta permanente.
>
> Venden objetos de segunda mano.
>
> Se celebra un día a la semana.
>
> Tiene tiendas en su interior.
>
> Está al aire libre, en plazas y calles.
>
> Se pueden encontrar puestos de venta de diversos objetos.

In the market in Toledo you can find almost everything. In the next activity somebody wants to buy a few pottery items.

Actividad 7.14

Listen to Extract 16 on the Interviews Cassette and write down the items this person wants to buy.

Ahora escuche el Extracto 16 de la Cinta de entrevistas y escriba lo que esta persona quiere comprar.

Actividad 7.15

Regatear (bargaining) is an important aspect of shopping in the *mercadillo*. Below is a list of the amounts of money mentioned in the conversation. Listen again to *Extracto 16* on the Interviews Cassette and link these amounts with the items they refer to.

Escuche otra vez la conversación y una los precios con los objetos.

500 pesetas	un frutero
700 pesetas	
1.000 pesetas	un jarrón
2.500 pesetas	
2.000 pesetas	unos juegos para consomé
1.800 pesetas	

Atando cabos

Pronombres y adjetivos demostrativos

There are six words (or their variants in gender and number) that keep cropping up during the conversation:

este, éste, ese, ése and *aquel, aquél*

With their appropriate feminine and plural forms, these are the demonstrative adjectives and the ones with accents are demonstrative pronouns: this, that, these, those.

Demonstrative adjectives are used to identify **which** objects are referred to (that is, to introduce nouns) while demonstrative pronouns **replace** the nouns.

The pronouns also differ from the adjectives in having an accent on the stressed syllable, as in:

> **Aquellos** *fruteros no.* **Aquéllos** *sí.*

> **Este** *plato es más barato que* **aquél.**

> **Este** *jarrón no es tan bonito como* **éste.**

Note that while English only defines two positions (here and there), Spanish has three:

Este, esta, estos, estas refer to what is close to the speaker.

Ese, esa, esos, esas refer to what is close to the person addressed.

Aquel, aquella, aquellos, aquellas refer to what is away from both the speaker and the person addressed.

Sometimes the expressions *de aquí* and *de allí* are used in addition to the adjective or pronoun, to emphasize where the objects are, as in:

> *Este libro de aquí.*   This book here.

> *Esas plantas de allí.*   Those plants there.

Actividad 7.16

Now turn to the transcript of Extract 16 (from '*¡Hola! ¿Me puedes enseñar aquel jarrón?*' up to '*No sé.*') and underline all the demonstrative adjectives or pronouns you find.

Vaya a la transcripción del Extracto 16 y subraye todos los demostrativos que encuentre.

Actividad 7.17

Look at the sketches below and complete the gaps in the sentences with the appropriate demonstrative adjectives or pronouns. Remember to check that the gender and number agree with the noun referred to.

Complete los espacios con los adjetivos o pronombres demostrativos que faltan.

1 Pásame ...... botas, por favor.

2 Prefiero ...... bañador a ......

3 ¿Puedo probarme ...... chaqueta?

4 ¿Cuánto vale ...... bolso?

5 No me gustan ...... pantalones.

6 ...... corbata es más barata que ......

7 ¿Me pasa ...... paquete, por favor?

Actividad 7.18

From the box below, make up pairs of words that can be linked by the preposition *de* (because of their purpose, the material they are made of, how they are used, and so on).

Una las siguientes palabras según su relación, ya sea en uso, material, etc., y únalas con la preposición 'de'.

Ejemplo

cinturón / piel ➜ un cinturón de piel

> gafas, seda, tienda, verano, guantes, camisa, pana, tarjeta, sol, comestibles, lana, billetera, cuero, pantalones, crédito, chaqueta, rebajas, piel

Vocabulary – building on words you know

When you learn new vocabulary, you need to learn words in their context, not on their own. Most words are used in particular contexts: that is, they frequently occur together with certain other words. By learning words in their context you will not only increase the extent of your vocabulary, but also use it more accurately.

Resumiendo...

Now you can:

- ask for and give opinions
- use numbers and count up to 2,000
- use an answering machine
- pronounce *b* and *v*
- use demonstrative pronouns and adjectives
- use vocabulary and expressions for shopping

Unidad 8 ¡Que te mejores!

This final *unidad* looks at health and how to talk about it. In the Audio
Drama, you can hear what happens to Teresa after her car accident. The final
interviews in Toledo are with a class of primary school children who talk
about their knowledge of health and sing a few songs about it.

Sección 1

The last episode of the Audio Drama is dominated by Teresa's car accident.
You will find out what happens to her and how things turn out in her
relationship.

Key learning points

- Enquiring and giving information about health

- Revising the perfect tense

- Learning vocabulary relating to health

Actividad 8.1 | Before you listen to the last episode of *El idioma del amor*, read the vocabulary in the box below. All the words have something to do with health. List them under the headings that follow.

Distribuya las siguientes palabras en las categorías a continuación.

> venda, médico, hospital, operación, ambulancia, jarabe, jeringuilla, escáner, dolor de cabeza, sanatorio, alergia, conmoción, herida, enfermera (,-o), pastillas, gripe, análisis, doctor, radiografía, Urgencias, catarro, pomada, pediatra, camilla, infección, quirófano, anestesista, enfermedad, estetoscopio, constipado, cirujano, fractura, bisturí, dentista, apendicitis, escayola, UVI (Unidad de Vigilancia Intensiva), inyección, termómetro

Instalaciones y transporte médico	Personal médico	Instrumental	Dolencias	Diagnóstico, remedios y medicamentos

Actividad 8.2 | **1** At the end of the previous episode of *El idioma del amor*, Teresa had a car accident. Now guess what happens afterwards. Tick what you think is going to happen in this episode. Do not look in the *Clave* yet.

Adivine qué ocurre después del accidente de Teresa. Marque lo que cree que va a ocurrir en este episodio.

(a) A Teresa no le ha pasado nada. ❏

(b) Teresa es trasladada al hospital. ❏

(c) Teresa se muere. ❏

(d) Teresa se recupera pronto. ❏

(e) Teresa está muy grave. ❏

(f) Omar no sabe nada del accidente. ❏

(g) La madre de Teresa se entera del accidente. ❏

(h) La madre de Teresa se siente responsable por lo que ha pasado. ❏

(i) La madre de Teresa culpa a Omar de lo que ha pasado. ❏

(j) Hay un final feliz. ❏

2 Now listen to Episode 8 and check whether your predictions were correct.

Ahora escuche el último episodio y compruebe si sus predicciones son correctas.

Actividad 8.3

Listen to Episode 8 again and choose the correct statement from each of these groups.

Escuche otra vez el Episodio 8 y elija de cada grupo la frase correcta.

1 (a) Omar lleva a Teresa al hospital. ❑

(b) Omar llama una ambulancia. ❑

(c) Omar pide que alguien llame una ambulancia. ❑

2 (a) Teresa recupera el conocimiento inmediatamente. ❑

(b) Teresa recupera el conocimiento al cabo de unas horas. ❑

(c) Teresa no recupera el conocimiento hasta el día siguiente. ❑

3 (a) Teresa está sola el primer día. ❑

(b) Omar y Carmen están con Teresa desde el primer momento. ❑

(c) Omar está con Teresa desde el primer momento. ❑

4 (a) Carmen le contó el accidente a doña Amelia. ❑

(b) Omar le contó el accidente a doña Amelia. ❑

(c) Doña Amelia se enteró del accidente porque la llamaron del hospital. ❑

5 (a) Teresa culpa a su madre de todo. ❑

(b) Doña Amelia no se siente responsable de nada. ❑

(c) Doña Amelia está arrepentida de su actitud. ❑

6 (a) La madre de Teresa no llora. ❑

(b) Teresa no llora. ❑

(c) Teresa y su madre lloran. ❑

Actividad 8.4

Now listen to the first part of Episode 8 (up to '… *alguien entra en la sala.*'). Try to find the words in the recording that match the definitions overleaf.

Escuche la primera parte del episodio e intente encontrar las palabras que corresponden a las siguientes definiciones.

1 vehículo para trasladar enfermos · · · · · ·

2 que ha perdido el sentido · · · · · ·

3 departamento de un hospital donde llevan a los pacientes
   que requieren atención inmediata · · · · · ·

4 rotura de un hueso · · · · · ·

5 reposar, no hacer nada · · · · · ·

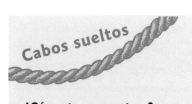

Cabos sueltos

¿Cómo te encuentras?

This is how you might enquire about somebody's health:

> *¿Cómo estás?*
>
> *¿Qué tal estás?*
>
> *¿Cómo te encuentras?*
>
> *¿Te encuentras bien?*
>
> *¿Te duele algo?*
>
> *¿Qué te duele?*
>
> *¿Qué te pasa?*

This is how to reply:

> *Estoy bien / mejor / peor.*
>
> *Me encuentro bien / mejor / peor.*
>
> *No me siento bien.*
>
> *Me duele la cabeza / el estómago.*
>
> *Estoy (un poco) mareado, -da.*
>
> *No tengo nada grave.*
>
> *No es nada.*

There are two ways of describing aches and pains:

> ***Me duele*** *la cabeza / el estómago / un pie / la espalda, etc.*
>
> ***Me duelen*** *las piernas / los oídos / las muelas / los riñones, etc.*
>
> ***Tengo dolor de***…

> While *me duele(n)* can be used for virtually every part of the body, the usage of *tengo dolor de* is more restricted. It is appropriate to use it, however, for the following:
>
> > *Tengo dolor de cabeza / garganta / estómago /*
> >
> > *oídos / espalda / muelas.*
>
> If you have no aches or pain at all, you can say:
>
> > *No me duele nada.*

Actividad 8.5

1   You will have heard Omar and Teresa talking about Teresa's health. Can you remember the phrases they use? If not, use the transcript to identify them.

¿Qué expresiones usan Omar y Teresa para hablar del estado de salud de Teresa?

2   What questions would you have to ask in order to get the following answers? Practise saying these questions aloud.

Practique en voz alta las preguntas que tendría que hacer para obtener las siguientes respuestas.

(a) Ya estoy mejor.

(b) Sí, gracias. Ya me he recuperado.

(c) He tenido un accidente.

(d) Nada, pero estoy un poco mareado, (-da).

(e) Sí, los oídos.

When Doña Amelia visits Teresa in hospital, they have a talk about recent events and other things in the past. They use the perfect tense, since what they are discussing either happened in the immediate past or still affects the present. Check *Atando cabos* in *Unidad 2, Actividad 2.2,* to revise the use of this tense.

Actividad 8.6

1   In the following conversation between Teresa and her mother the perfect tenses have been omitted. Fill in the gaps with the appropriate verb from the box below. The first one has been done for you.

Complete el siguiente texto con la forma del verbo correspondiente.

> ver, pensar, pasar, ser, servir, enterarse, ver, terminar, ser, sufrir, pedir

Madre ¡Hija, no sabes cuánto siento lo que ...ha pasado...!

Teresa [...] Pero, ¿cómo te ....?

Madre Llamé a tu piso y Carmen me lo dijo. La .... abajo.

Teresa ¿No .... a Omar?

Madre Sí. Y le .... perdón por todo. Ya sabes: ....una estúpida. [...]

[...]

Madre [...] .... mucho sobre todo lo ocurrido, ¿sabes? [...] Sabes lo que .... contigo desde que te quedaste embarazada. [...] Pero eso .... una equivocación. Ahora sé que sólo .... para hacerte sufrir más.

Teresa Mamá, no importa ya. Todo eso ....

2   Now listen to the rest of the episode, then check what you have written in the Transcript Booklet. Note that we only included sentences in the perfect tense.

Ahora escuche el resto del episodio y compruebe lo que ha escrito con la transcripción.

Now that you have heard the whole Audio Drama, let's see how much you remember of the story. You might want to listen to parts of it again, or even all of it if you have time!

Actividad 8.7

1   How many facts about Spanish life can you recall from the drama? To find out, answer the questions below in English.

¿De qué información cultural que aparece en el Radiodrama se acuerda? Conteste en inglés las siguientes preguntas para averiguarlo.

(a) ¿Cómo se llaman las películas que van a ver Omar y Teresa?

(b) ¿Qué actriz y qué directores de cine se mencionan?

(c) ¿Qué lenguas cooficiales hay en España además del castellano?

(d) ¿De qué pintor hablan Omar y Teresa después de visitar el Museo del Prado?

(e) ¿Qué tipo de tienda tiene la madre de Teresa?

(f) ¿Cómo se llama una de las estaciones de tren en Madrid?

2   In the Audio Drama there are some moments of greater dramatic tension than others. Mark the graph opposite to show tension levels in each episode, as you perceived them.

Complete el siguiente gráfico indicando cuáles fueron para usted los momentos de mayor tensión dramática.

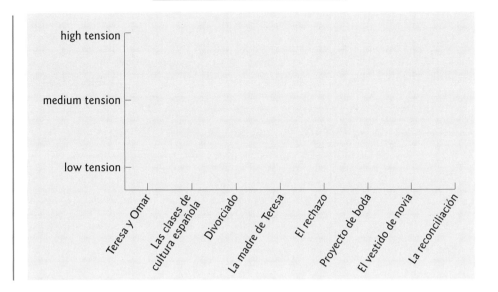

Sección 2

There is an old saying in Spanish: *Más vale prevenir que curar*. This *sección* looks at some possible preventive measures against a certain illness. You will also be learning about some common ailments, together with remedies and advice for dealing with them.

> **Key learning points**
> - Giving advice
> - Using the imperative (distinguishing between advice, orders and instructions)
> - Study skills: inferring the meaning of new vocabulary

Actividad 8.8

Use the names of the parts of the body to label the drawings overleaf.

Ponga los nombres de las partes del cuerpo en los dibujos.

> cabeza, cara, nariz, oreja, pecho, cuello, brazo, ojo, codo, mano, boca.dedo de la mano, hombro, estómago, cintura, cadera, pierna, tobillo, pie, dedo del pie

El cuerpo humano

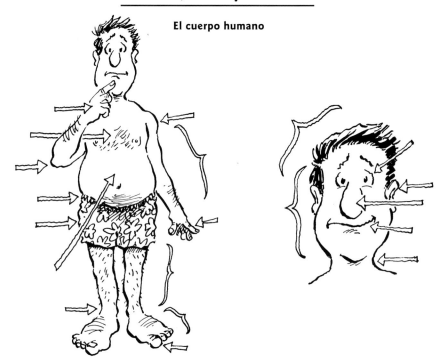

Actividad 8.9

Read the article below, which deals with osteoporosis, a medical condition.

Lea el siguiente texto.

masa ósea
bone tissue
achacarse a
to be attributed to
diagnóstico precoz
early diagnosis

Inferring the meaning of new vocabulary

The article you are about to read is quite specialized and has difficult vocabulary. You can deal with this by using various clues to deduce the meaning. First try to predict what the article is going to be about by making sure you understand the title and subtitle. Then you may be able to guess the meaning of unfamiliar words, either by looking at their immediate context or by comparing them with similar words in your own (or another) language.

OSTEOPOROSIS

Una enfermedad en aumento

La osteoporosis se caracteriza por una fragilidad en los huesos que tiene como consecuencia a largo plazo la aparición de fracturas ante mínimos esfuerzos, como puede ser simplemente estornudar. Pero, ¿cómo se puede llegar a esa situación?

El hueso es un tejido vivo que se encuentra en constante renovación. Es decir, nuestro organismo está continuamente destruyendo y consptruyendo pequeñas áreas de tejido óseo. Este proceso está controlado por diversas hormonas. En los primeros años de la vida adulta, la masa ósea aumenta hasta alcanzar su máximo, es decir, se construye más hueso del que se destruye. Después se produce un período de estabilidad, tras el cual comienza una fase en la que la destrucción del tejido óseo es mayor que la formación de hueso.

Este desequilibrio, que comienza a partir de los 35–40 años, se acentúa de forma exagerada tras la menopausia en las mujeres, ya que los ovarios cesan su actividad hormonal y disminuyen los niveles de estrógenos. Sin embargo, esta pérdida de masa ósea puede pasar totalmente desapercibida y se suele diagnosticar cuando aparece la primera fractura de hueso. El tratamiento en esta fase es muy difícil, porque la pérdida de masa ósea es ya demasiado grande. De ahí la importancia de detectar con antelación los factores de riesgo de la osteoporosis.

La osteoporosis puede producir algunos síntomas como dolor, pérdida de altura y deformidades. Sin embargo, estos signos suelen achacarse muchas veces al proceso natural de envejecimiento y no suelen tomarse en consideración. Actualmente es posible hacer un diagnóstico precoz, gracias al perfeccionamiento de la tecnología existente y al desarrollo de nuevos métodos de diagnóstico.

(Basado en un artículo aparecido en *Clara*, febrero de 1995, p. 44)

2   Now read the article again and answer, in Spanish, the following questions.

Ahora vuelva a leer el artículo y conteste en español las siguientes preguntas.

(a) ¿Cuál es la consecuencia más obvia de la osteoporosis a largo plazo?

(b) ¿Qué se entiende por 'constante renovación del tejido óseo'?

(c) ¿Cuándo deja de aumentar la masa ósea?

(d) ¿Por qué afecta la osteoporosis principalmente a las mujeres de mediana edad?

(e) ¿Por qué es importante hacer un diagnóstico temprano de la osteoporosis?

(f) ¿Cómo empieza a manifestarse la osteoporosis?

(g) ¿Por qué no suelen tomarse en consideración los síntomas de la osteoporosis?

(h) ¿Qué avances médicos ha habido en este campo?

Cabos sueltos

Dar consejos

People often offer advice to those who are ill. There are several different ways of giving advice, reflecting various levels of insistence:

- Using the imperative:

   Toma estas pastillas.   Take these pills.

   Acuéstate.   Go to bed.

   Ve al dentista.   Go and see the dentist.

- Using *tener que*:

   Tienes que tomar estas pastillas.   You must take these pills.

   Tienes que acostarte.   You have to go to bed.

   Tienes que ir al dentista.   You must go and see the dentist.

- Using *deber* (slightly less forceful):

   Debes tomar estas pastillas.   You ought to take these pills.

   Debes acostarte.   You should go to bed.

   Debes ir al dentista.   You had better see a dentist.

Actividad 8.10

1 The people in the sketches below all have some ailment. Look at them and listen to Extract 24 (part one) on the Activities Cassette. Number the pictures in the same order as the descriptions in the audio extract. (You might also want to practise saying that you're suffering from these ailments in Extract 24 (part two).)

Mire los dibujos y escuche el Extracto 24 (primera parte) de la Cinta de actividades. Numere los dibujos según aparecen en la cinta. También puede practicar cómo expresar estas dolencias en el Extracto 24: segunda parte.

2 Give the sufferers some advice on how to get better. Look at the pairs of words below, and write sentences appropriate to each condition. Use one of the forms given in the *Cabos sueltos*.

Deles consejo, usando las expresiones de 'Cabos sueltos'. Escriba las frases apropiadas.

> tomar/jarabe   ir/dentista   tomar/aspirina
> tomar/manzanilla   acostarse/descansar

3 Now listen to Extract 25 (part one) on the Activities Cassette and give advice to people with different health problems.

Ahora escuche la cinta y dé consejo a unas personas con diferentes problemas de salud.

Cabos sueltos

If you want to tell someone that you hope they will get better, use the following expressions:

> *¡Cuídate!*   Take care of yourself.
>
> *¡Que te mejores!*   Get well soon.

Actividad 8.11

You will now practise the use of the imperative. It can be used to give advice, instructions or commands. The meaning of the sentence will normally tell you which is intended, but the intonation pattern of the sentence can also provide a clue.

1   Read the sentences below and note whether you think they are *un consejo, una instrucción* or *una orden.*

Lea las siguientes frases y diga si cree que son consejos, instrucciones u órdenes.

(a) Debes ir al hospital.

(b) ¡Acuéstate ahora mismo!

(c) Antes de tomar el jarabe, agita bien el frasco.

(d) ¡No tomes más jarabe!

(e) Toma estas pastillas, son muy buenas para el dolor de cabeza.

(f) ¡Llama una ambulancia!

(g) Échate un poco de pomada en la quemadura.

(h) Haz movimientos circulares con el cuello cada noche.

2   Now listen to Extract 26 on the Activities Cassette. Check the meaning of each sentence by listening for its intonation and repeat it in the gap provided.

Escuche las frases y repítalas en las pausas imitando la entonación.

Activity 8.12

Children's rhymes and riddles are useful for learning Spanish pronunciation and a good aid to memorizing. Listen to the children's rhyme on Extract 27 on the Activities Cassette. Repeat it after the model and try to imitate its pronunciation and rhythm.

Escuche una rima infantil en el Extracto 27 de la Cinta de actividades y repítala después del modelo. Fíjese en la pronunciación y el ritmo.

Sección 3

In this last *sección* we will hear children talking about parts of the body and illnesses. They also talk about the different senses and explain what they are for. Finally, you can have a look at the report the doctor wrote about Teresa when she was admitted to hospital.

Key learning points

- Building vocabulary for parts of the body
- Suggesting remedies
- Study skills: proof-reading

Actividad 8.13

Match the following descriptions with the words in the box below. If you cannot complete the activity, use a dictionary.

Una las siguientes definiciones con las palabras del recuadro. Use el diccionario si no puede completar el ejercicio.

> uñas, dientes, párpados, hígado, barbilla, cejas, corazón, labios, pulmones, frente, muñeca, riñones, lengua, mejillas, ombligo, pestañas

1 Son dos órganos internos situados en la parte trasera del cuerpo, cerca de la cintura.

2 Es la parte de abajo de la cara.

3 Tenemos veinte en el cuerpo.

4 Une la mano al brazo.

5 Es como un botón en medio del cuerpo.

6 Los usamos para morder.

7 Sin ella, no podemos hablar.

8 Es un órgano interno, que está a la derecha del estómago.

9 Tenemos dos en la cara, a ambos lados de la nariz.

10 Los usamos para cerrar los ojos.

11 Es el órgano que bombea la sangre.

12 Tenemos dos, encima de los ojos.

13 Tenemos dos y forman la parte externa de la boca.

14 Tenemos muchas, alrededor de los ojos.

15 El aire que respiramos va a estos órganos.

16 Es la parte de arriba de la cara.

Actividad 8.14

Listen to Extract 17 on the Interviews Cassette. Then add words from the box to the column on the right to match the descriptions.

Escuche el Extracto 17 de la Cinta de entrevistas y escriba las palabras del recuadro en la columna correspondiente de la derecha.

1	Son articulaciones	
2	Son extremidades	
3	Están en la mano	
4	Están en la cabeza	
5	Está en la parte de atrás	

Culo is a colloquial term for 'backside'.

pulgar, nudillos, espalda, índice, brazos, dientes, codo, cerebro, culo, piernas

Curiosidad ~

En español se usa la misma palabra, 'dedo', con los significados *finger* y *toe*. Sin embargo, se puede diferenciar entre 'dedos de la mano' y 'dedos del pie'. Para designar el dedo gordo de la mano y del pie, se suele usar la palabra 'pulgar'.

Actividad 8.15

In the sketches below, the arrows point to various parts of the body mentioned by the children. Listen again to Extract 17 on the Interviews Cassette and add the appropriate label to each arrow.

Escuche otra vez la cinta y escriba los nombres de las partes del cuerpo junto a las flechas.

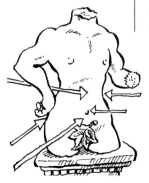

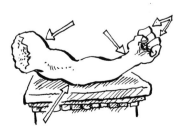

Actividad 8.16

The children also talk about the five senses and what they are for. They relate them to different parts of the body. Listen to Extract 18 on the Interviews Cassette and, from the columns below, match the parts of the body with the senses and the functions of that part of the body.

Una las partes del cuerpo con los sentidos y sus funciones.

ojos	sirven para ver	el gusto
nariz	sirven para tocar	el oído
oídos	sirven para oír	la vista
boca	sirve para oler	el tacto
manos	sirve para saborear	el olfato

Dar remedios

The preposition *para* here indicates function or purpose. This preposition is often used when talking about remedies: *es bueno, (-a), para...* or *va(n) bien para...*

La miel **es buena para** la tos.   Honey is good for a cough.
La miel **va bien para** la tos.

Los masajes **son buenos para**   Massages are good for backache.
el dolor de espalda.
Los masajes **van bien para**
el dolor de espalda.

Actividad 8.17

Here is the doctor's report on Teresa. Unfortunately, the new secretary is still not used to the doctor's handwriting, and every now and then he types the wrong word. Read the report and correct it. There are seven mistakes in words relating to health.

He aquí un informe de la doctora sobre el estado de salud de Teresa. Lea el informe y corríjalo.

Proof-reading

What you are about to do is a kind of proof-reading. Whenever you write anything in Spanish, try to look over it again in this way. Many words look very similar to one another but have a different meaning. When you next write something, read the draft a couple of times to check for misspellings and possible misunderstandings.

Hospital de Santa Mercedes

Miércoles, 3 de octubre de 1998

La pariente Teresa Martínez ha ingresado
esta mañana en el destacamento de
Urgencias. La enferma tenía conmoción y
llegó incontinente, pero pasadas unas horas
se ha recuperado. Esta tarde se le ha
puesto el terremoto y tiene un poco de
fiebre. Después del examen no se ha
encontrado ninguna factura. Tiene un
pequeño porte en la cabeza, pero no es nada
grave. Le he recetado unos sedantes para el
color de cabeza.

> Dra. Remedios de Sastre.

Actividad 8.18

The following anagrams and word puzzles refer to health and parts of the body. You will have to use different techniques to work out what they are.

1 Order the letters to form words to refer to parts of the body.

Ordene las letras para formar palabras relacionadas con partes del cuerpo.

traganga	gobomli	tógomesa	erpain
baceaz	soheu	resiñon	

2 Order the syllables to form words referring to installations, personnel and medical instruments.

Ordene las sílabas para obtener palabras relacionadas con instalaciones, personal e instrumental médico.

cia-bu-lan-am	tal-hos-pi	lla-mi-ca
or-doct	ra-en-me-fer	

3 Add the appropriate vowels to form words concerned with ailments.

Añada las vocales que faltan para obtener las palabras sobre dolencias.

fr__ct__r__   d__l__r   __l__rg__ __

4 Substitute the correct letter to replace the letter ñ to form words related to diagnosis and remedies.

Sustituya la letra 'ñ' con la letra correspondiente para obtener palabras relacionadas con diagnosis y remedios.

jarañe   reñoso   pastiña

rañiografía   oñeración

Resumiendo...

Now you can:

- enquire and give information about health

- give advice, orders and instructions

- use the imperative in the *tú* form

- make suggestions

- use vocabulary relating to parts of the body

Resumen gramatical

Articles

There are two types of articles: definite (el/la/los/las) and indefinite (un/una/unos/unas). The English equivalents are 'the'and 'a' ('an').

Articles in Spanish agree both in gender and number with the noun they accompany:

	Definite		Indefinite	
	Singular	Plural	Singular	Plural
Masculine	**el** niño	**los** niños	**un** niño	**unos** niños
Feminine	**la** casa	**las** casas	**una** casa	**unas** casas

Nouns

Nouns are names of persons, animals, objects, places, ideas or events. They may be unique to one individual (Mary) or define a kind (a girl).

Gender

In Spanish, nouns are either masculine *(el niño)* or feminine *(la niña)*. There are ways of knowing which:

- most nouns ending in *–o* are **masculine**: *el barco*
- most nouns ending in *–a* are **feminine**: *la camisa*
- there are a few exceptions, such as: **la mano, el día, el mapa, el** *monarca*
- some nouns end in *–e* or in *–ista* or a consonant: these might be either feminine or masculine, and need to be learned: **el** *coche,* **el** *dentista,* **el** *camión*
- nouns that can refer to either men or women, such as the names of professions, can have both masculine and feminine forms: *el camarero, la camarera.*

Number

Nouns have both singular *(el niño / la niña)* and plural forms *(los niños / las niñas).* There are rules for forming the plural:

- nouns ending in a vowel add *-s (billete* ➔ *billetes)*
- nouns ending in a consonant add *-es (tren* ➔ *trenes)*
- there are some exceptions to this rule: *las gafas* ('spectacles') is always plural, while *la gente* ('people') is usually singular.

Pronouns

Pronouns substitute nouns to avoid repetition. Personal pronouns refer specifically to people, or sometimes to animals.

Pronouns vary according to their role in the sentence. Subject pronouns replace the nouns for the **subject** of the verb (***Raquel** lleva gafas* ➔ ***Ella** lleva gafas*); direct object pronouns replace the **object** of the verb (*Miguel escribe **un libro*** ➔ *Miguel **lo** escribe*); indirect object pronouns replace indirect objects (*Yo **les** doy consejos*).

Subject pronouns		Direct object pronouns		Indirect object pronouns	
yo	*I*	me	*me*	me	*to me*
tú (inf. sing.)	*you*	te (inf. sing.)	*you*	te (inf. sing.)	*to you*
Ud. (frml. sing.)	*you*	lo/la	*you (frml. sing.)*	le (frml. sing.)	*to you*
él/ella	*he/she/it*	lo/la	*him/her/it*	le	*to him/ to her/to it*
nosotros,-as	*we*	nos	*us*	nos	*to us*
vosotros,-as (inf. pl.)	*you*	os (inf. pl.)	*you*	os (inf. pl.)	*to you*
Uds. (frml. pl.)	*you*	los/las (frml. pl.)	*you*	les (frml. pl.)	*to you*
ellos/ellas	*they*	los/las	*them*	les	*to them*

Question words

¿Qué...?   *What?*

¿Quién...?   *Who?*

¿Dónde...?   *Where?*

¿Cuándo...?   *When?*

¿Por qué...?   *Why?*

¿Cómo...?   *How?*

¿Cuánto, -a...?   *How much?*

¿Cuántos, -as...?   *How many?*

Note that a preposition may be put before any of these interrogative pronouns:

¿Por dónde se va a…?	*How do I get to…?*
¿A cuántos kilómetros está…?	*How many kilometres away is…?*
¿Para qué van Teresa y Omar a…?	*Why are Teresa and Omar going to…?*
¿En qué van Teresa y Omar a…?	*How do Teresa and Omar get to…?*

Verbs

Present tense

There are three different groups of verbs in Spanish, those ending respectively in *–ar (trabajar), –er (comer)* and *–ir (vivir).* The present tense is formed by appending the appropriate first-, second- or third-person endings to the stem of the verb, as shown in bold below:

	trabaj**AR**	com**ER**	viv**IR**
(yo)	trabaj**o**	com**o**	viv**o**
(tú)	trabaj**as**	com**es**	viv**es**
(él/ella/Ud.)	trabaj**a**	com**e**	viv**e**
(nosotros,-as)	trabaj**amos**	com**emos**	viv**imos**
(vosotros,-as)	trabaj**áis**	com**éis**	viv**ís**
(ellos/ellas/Uds.)	trabaj**an**	com**en**	viv**en**

In some verbs the middle vowel of the stem changes in all but the *nosotros* and *vosotros* forms *(querer→quiero).* These are called 'radical changing verbs'. Here are a few more:

emp**e**zar	→	emp**ie**zo
s**e**guir	→	s**i**go
d**o**rmir	→	d**ue**rmo
j**u**gar	→	j**ue**go
ac**o**star	→	ac**ue**sto

The common irregular verbs *ser* and *estar* may both translate as 'to be' but have distinct uses:

	Ser	Estar
(yo)	soy	estoy
(tú)	eres	estás
(él/ella/Ud.)	es	está
(nosotros,–as)	somos	estamos
(vosotros,–as)	sois	estáis
(ellos/ellas/Uds.)	son	están

Ser is used:

- to talk about nationalities
- to state your job
- to talk about time
- to describe characteristic features of persons
- to describe features of a place

Estar is used:

- to indicate location
- to describe moods and temporary characteristics
- to talk about the weather
- to give marital status
- to talk about temporary state of health

The verb *gustar*

The verb *gustar* has a different construction from the English equivalent ('to like'). It actually means 'to be pleasing to', as in *Me gusta el arte* ('Art is pleasing to me').

Me gusta el arte abstracto. Me gustan los cuadros de Picasso.

Te gusta el Parque del Retiro. Te gustan las obras de Miró.

Le gusta Diego Rivera. Le gustan los museos.

Nos gusta Miró. Nos gustan las esculturas.

Os gusta Goya. Os gustan los murales mexicanos.

Les gusta el arte cubista. Les gustan las fotografías.

Pronominal verbs

These verbs are formed by including the object pronouns *me, te, se, nos, os, se.* They are therefore conjugated as below:

(yo)	**me** levanto	(nosotros,–as)	**nos** levantamos
(tú)	**te** levantas	(vosotros,–as)	**os** levantáis
(él/ella/Ud.)	**se** levanta	(ellos/ellas/Uds.)	**se** levantan

The verb endings are conjugated in the usual way, depending on whether they end in *–ar, –er* or *–ir* in the infinitive.

Describing a process with *se* + third person verb

When it is not necessary to mention the person (or thing) carrying out an activity, we can use the impersonal expression: '*se* + third person'. One of the uses of this construction is to give instructions.

Se pela la fruta.   *The fruit is peeled.*

Se cortan las manzanas.   *The apples are cut / diced.*

Note that if an object pronoun is used, it will be placed between the pronoun *se* and the verb, for example:

Se **le** añaden los huevos.   *The eggs are added **to it**.*

Perfect tense

The perfect tense is used to talk about what people **have done**. Here is how you form it:

		past participles*		
		cantar	comer	vivir
(yo)	he	cantado	comido	vivido
(tú)	has	cantado	comido	vivido
(él/ella/Ud.)	ha	cantado	comido	vivido
(nosotros,–as)	hemos	cantado	comido	vivido
(vosotros,–as)	habéis	cantado	comido	vivido
(ellos/ellas/Uds.)	han	cantado	comido	vivido

* Some irregular past participles are: *hecho (hacer), roto (romper), puesto (poner), vuelto (volver), dicho (decir), muerto (morir).*

Future with *ir a*

Ir a + infinitive is similar to the English 'to be going to do something'. It is often used to describe a planned future action:

(yo)	voy		
(tú)	vas		
(él/ella/Ud.)	va		
(nosotros,–as)	vamos	+ a + viajar	
(vosotros,–as)	vais		
(ellos/ellas/Uds.)	van		

Gerund

The gerund form in Spanish corresponds to the '–ing' form in English. The gerunds of regular verbs are formed as follows:

> *–ar* verbs (*pasear, escuchar*) add *–ando* to the stem   *paseando*

> *–er* verbs (*beber, comer*) add *–iendo* to the stem   *bebiendo*

> *–ir* verbs (*salir, vivir*) add *–iendo* to the stem   *saliendo*

There are a few irregular forms, such as:

> leer → leyendo

> caer → cayendo

> dormir → durmiendo

> pedir → pidiendo

> ir → yendo

The gerund is also used to form the present continuous (see below).

Present continuous

If you want to express **continuous** action in Spanish, you do so in the same way as in English, by using the present continuous. It is formed from *estar* (past, present or future form) plus the gerund:

> **Estoy leyendo** un libro.   *I am reading a book.*

The imperative

The imperative form of the verb can be used for giving orders, advice or instructions.

Opposite is how you form the imperative in the *tú* and *vosotros* forms.

Singular (*tú*)	Plural (from the infinitive)
tomas ➔ **toma**	toma **r** ➔ **tomad**
comes ➔ **come**	come **r** ➔ **comed**
subes ➔ **sube**	subi **r** ➔ **subid**

There are a few irregular imperatives in the *tú* form:

salir ➔ sal		tener ➔ ten	
poner ➔ pon		venir ➔ ven	
decir ➔ di		ir ➔ ve	
hacer ➔ haz			

Adverbs and adverbial expressions

nunca   *never*

casi nunca   *almost never*

a veces   *sometimes*

frecuentemente / con frecuencia   *frequently*

siempre   *always*

Adjectives

Adjectival agreement and position

In Spanish, adjectives (*antiguo, artístico*) agree in gender and number with the nouns they describe and usually follow them:

Es un apartamento **ordenado** y **limpio.**

Es una ciudad **interesantísima**.

However, the masculine singular adjectives *bueno, malo, primero, tercero* and *grande* can be used before the noun in the forms: *buen, mal, primer, tercer* and *gran*.

Comparative adjectives

más moderno **que**   *more modern than*

menos moderno **que**   *less modern than*

tan moderno **como**   *as modern as*

Some adjectives have an irregular comparative form:

bueno *(good)* ➔ mejor *(better)*   *El ordenador es mejor que la máquina de escribir.*

malo *(bad)* ➔ peor *(worse)*   *El teléfono es peor que el correo electrónico.*

Superlative adjectives

Superlatives are formed by adding *el, la, los, las* to the comparatives *más* or *menos*:

el (buzón) **más** cerca de aquí   *the nearest (postbox) to here*

la (ciudad) **menos** ruidosa   *the least noisy (city)*

los (sobres) **más** caros   *the most expensive (envelopes)*

las (libretas) **más** baratas   *the cheapest (notebooks)*

There are also some irregular forms:

el/la/lo mejor   *the best*

el/la/lo peor   *the worst*

el/la/lo mayor   *the eldest / largest*

el/la/lo menor   *the youngest / smallest*

Demonstratives

Demonstrative **adjectives** are used to introduce nouns, while demonstrative **pronouns** replace nouns. Demonstrative **pronouns** also differ from demonstrative **adjectives** in that they have an accent on the stressed syllable.

Este / Éste refers to what is close to the speaker.

Ese / Ése refers to what is close to the person addressed.

Aquel / Aquél refers to what is away from both the speaker and the person addressed.

	Masculine	Feminine	Masculine	Feminine	Masculine	Feminine
Singular	Este/Éste	Esta/Ésta	Ese/Ése	Esa/Ésa	Aquel/ Aquél	Aquella/ Aquélla
Plural	Estos/Éstos	Estas/Éstas	Esos/Ésos	Esas/Ésas	Aquellos/ Aquéllos	Aquellas/ Aquéllas

Prepositions

Here are some of the most common prepositions:

- a *(direction, destination or time)*   Carmen y Mercedes van a Cancún.

- hasta *(space or time limit)*   El autocar no para hasta Barcelona.

- para *(direction or time)*   Este camión va para el centro.

- de *(coming from)*   Es el tren de cercanías.

- por *(movement within certain limits through, or to express time)*
  El camión pasa por la Avenida de la Reforma.

- en *(location in time or space)*   Los servicios se encuentran en la vía.

- con *(showing who you are with, or what you do something with)*
  ¿Con quién viajas?

- al fondo *(at the back)*

- en el centro *(in the middle)*

- enfrente *(opposite, facing)*

- entre *(among, between)*

- sobre, en, encima (de) *(on, on top of)*

- detrás (de) *(behind)*

- delante (de) *(in front (of))*

- al lado (de) *(beside, next to)*

- dentro (de) *(inside, within)*

Personal *a*

When the direct object of a verb is a named or specific person or animal, it is preceded by *a*:

He visto **a** un amigo.

¿Conocéis **a** Miguel?

¿Conocéis España?

Negation

no and *nunca*

If you want to put a verb into the negative, whether it is in a simple or a compound tense or has any associated object pronouns, place *no* before the verb (or the pronoun / verb group):

Belén y Pablo **no han comprado** los billetes todavía.

Nunca means 'never' and in Spanish (unlike English) it requires a verb in its negative form:

No he ido **nunca** a Guatemala.

However, when *nunca* comes first in the sentence, the verb does not require *no*:

Nunca he ido a Guatemala.

lave

Actividad 1.1

Here are the greetings you would use at the times shown:

¡Buenos días!: 6.00, 09.30, 11.00, 12.15

¡Buenas tardes!: 15.45, 18.00

¡Buenas noches!: 21.30, 23.00, 00.15

Actividad 1.2

1   Formally. (They use *usted* and not *tú*.)

2   No. (They've just met.)

3   They are in a cinema queue in Madrid.

Actividad 1.3

1   (a) Yo me llamo Omar.

2   Here are the phrases you should have used for the different situations:

(a) (Yo) Me llamo… / Soy…

(b) Le presento al señor Martínez / Éste es el señor Martínez.

(c) Te presento a mi compañera / Ésta es Ana.

(d) Encantado (*if you are male*) / Encantada (*if you are female*) / Mucho gusto.

Actividad 1.4

1   Quedan en la puerta del cine.

2   Here are the expressions Teresa and Omar use to arrange to meet:

Omar   […] ¿A qué hora quedamos*?*

Teresa   ¿Le parece bien…?

Omar   Muy bien…

3   Here are the expressions they used to say good-bye:

Teresa   […] Hasta mañana…

Omar   Adiós, hasta mañana.

Actividad 1.5

1 The four words that are names of jobs are: *actor, ingeniero, profesor* and *cocinero*.

2 Below are the equivalent feminine forms of these professions.

Masculino	Femenino
actor	actriz
ingeniero	ingeniero / ingeniera
profesor	profesora
cocinero	cocinera

Actividad 1.6

2 You should have ticked:

(a) How old she is.

(b) Where she lives.

(c) Where she comes from.

(g) What her mother's name is.

3 Here are the descriptions of Teresa and Omar with the correct information in bold:

Teresa tiene **treinta y cuatro** años. Tiene **una hija (Carmen)**. Vive en **Madrid**. Trabaja en **la Escuela Oficial de Idiomas**. Es profesora de **inglés**. Su madre, doña Amelia, vive en **Toledo** y es **viuda**.

Omar tiene **treinta y cuatro** años. Es **alto**. Vive en Madrid, pero es de **Marruecos**. **Es ingeniero**, pero trabaja de **cocinero**. Quiere aprender **más sobre la cultura y la civilización españolas**. Su madre **murió**. **Era española**.

Actividad 1.7

1 The forms needed in the first person singular are: *me llamo, tengo, vivo, trabajo, soy, quiero*.

Your paragraph might look like this:

Me llamo Julia Stevens y tengo treinta y cinco años. Vivo en Londres y trabajo en una compañía de seguros. Soy contable. Quiero aprender español.

Actividad 1.8

2 Here is how the identity cards should look. The missing information is in bold.

CARNET DE IDENTIDAD N. 0055903

Apellidos: Martínez
Nombre: Teresa
Nacionalidad: española
Profesión: profesora
Estado civil: soltera
Lugar de nacimiento: Toledo
Domicilio: c/ Cava Alta, 23. Madrid.

CARNET DE IDENTIDAD N. 0075452

Apellidos: Boussidi
Nombre: Omar
Nacionalidad: marroquí
Profesión: ingeniero
Estado civil: divorciado
Lugar de nacimiento: Casablanca, Marruecos.
Domicilio: c/ Marqués de Santa Ana, 2. Madrid.

---

3 Here is a possible way of completing the visa form:

ESPAÑA MINISTERIO DE ASUNTOS EXTERIORES	SOLICITUD DE VISADO: ....

MISIÓN DIPLOMÁTICA U OFICINA CONSULAR:

1. APELLIDOS _López_
2. OTROS APELLIDOS _Johnson_
3. NOMBRES _Lisa_   4. SEXO _Mujer_
5. LUGAR Y FECHA DE NACIMIENTO _Nueva York, 31/07/63_
6. PAÍS _Estados Unidos_
7. NACIONALIDAD/ES ACTUAL/ES _EE UU_   8. ESTADO CIVIL _Casada_

Actividad 1.9

1 The following reasoning might help you in making your choice:

(a) Jesús offers formal Spanish lessons in exchange for English ones. He is also a languages graduate, so he will be able to help you with the grammar. Maybe that is what you prefer. Can you offer the same?

(b) Mercedes wants to practise her English. Maybe she can also help you with your Spanish, since she says she is a native Spanish speaker. She seems to speak some English, which could be an advantage if you don't speak any Spanish! Moreover, you can phone her at any time.

(c) If you are more interested in just conversation practice, Marta could be your choice. She is also a student of English, so will probably sympathize with your language problems.

2 Here is a description of the two people. Yours might, of course, be slightly different, but check that you have used the correct verbs: *ser*, *llevar* and *tener*.

María tiene unos treinta y cinco años. Es morena y alta. Lleva una camisa a rayas y pantalones vaqueros.

Rosa es una chica joven de unos veinte años. Es rubia y baja. Lleva pantalones vaqueros y gafas

Actividad 1.10

3 The names spelt on the cassette are: *Ortega, Villarino, Echevarría, Vaquero, Casals, Jiménez.*

Actividad 1.11

1 The British person is called Craig Irving.

3 (a) Juanjo Montalbán.

(b) La parada de metro de Lavapiés.

Actividad 1.13

1 Check your answers against the map (see opposite):

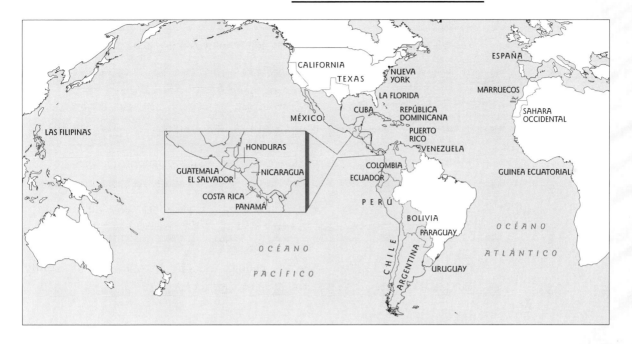

2 Here is the full table, with the completed information in bold:

Soy de... Inglaterra	Soy... inglés/inglesa	Hablo... inglés
Rusia	ruso / rusa	ruso
Francia	francés / francesa	**francés**
Italia	**italiano / italiana**	italiano
Suecia	**sueco / sueca**	**sueco**
Alemania	alemán / alemana	**alemán**
Estados Unidos	estadounidense	**inglés**
Marruecos	**marroquí**	**árabe**

Actividad 1.14

1 The two quotations suggest that Toledo is a city with a very rich history and influences from the East, particularly the Arab world.

2 Here are the adjectives that you might have ticked:

pequeña   (Toledo is quite a small city.)

artística   (The city possesses many national heritage buildings and museums.)

exótica   (The quotations and the *Curiosidad* say that Toledo has a connection with the Arab world.)

provinciana   (Toledo is not a big city.)

histórica	(Toledo reflects the complete history of Spain, according to one of the quotations.)
antigua	(Toledo has many old buildings.)
famosa	(Toledo is one of the most famous cities in Spain for the richness of its cultural heritage.)
turística	(Toledo is one of the most visited cities in Spain.)

The other adjectives (*industrial, despoblada, desconocida, costera*) do not really describe Toledo.

Actividad 1.15

(a) Granada – (ii)

(b) Cuzco – (iii)

(c) Madrid – (i)

Actividad 1.16

1 Your sentence could look like this:

Toledo es una ciudad histórica y famosa.

2 The adjectives from the list mentioned in the recording are:

medieval	('Es **medieval** y tiene calles pequeñas…')
antiguo	('… es una ciudad **antigua**.')
famoso	('¿Por qué es tan **famosa** Toledo?')
importante	('… donde vivieron nobles **importantes** de la antigüedad.')
bonito	('… tiene […] edificios muy **bonitos**…')
pequeño	('… tiene calles **pequeñas**…')

3 In the complete transcript below, the correct adjectives are in bold:

— ¿Cómo es Toledo?

— Es muy **bonita** porque es una ciudad antigua. Es **medieval** y tiene calles **pequeñas** y edificios muy bonitos, antiguos.

— ¿Por qué es tan **famosa** Toledo?

— ¿Toledo? Famosa por supuesto, por su historia, por su arte. Toda ella es historia y es arte.

— Es famosa, además por sus monumentos **artísticos**, porque han pasado muchas culturas por aquí. Ha habido árabes, judíos, cristianos… y es un centro de unión de gentes de pueblos **diversos**.

— ¿Qué hay para visitar?

— Está la catedral de Toledo, que es muy bonita, del siglo **gótico**, ¿eh? Luego tienes por ejemplo también el Alcázar, San Juan de los Reyes, que es un monasterio. Hay palacios donde vivieron nobles **importantes** de la antigüedad.

4 Here is the complete text, with the nouns described by the adjectives in bold italics and the correct endings in bold.

La ciudad de México, uno de los mayores *focos* cultural**es** de América Latina, es hoy *una* **gran** *urbe* modern**a** que concentra más de 20 millones de habitantes . En sus calles se entremezclan pasado, presente y futuro. La *plaza* del Zócalo, la más grande y antigu**a** de la ciudad, el Castillo de Chapultepec, el maravilloso *Museo* Arqueológic**o**, obra maestra de culturas milenarias, la *Zona* Rosa, área peatonal y donde se encuentran unos *comercios* muy lujos**os**, o el bonit**o** *barrio* de Coayacán donde vivió la famos**a** *pintora* Frida Kahlo y su esposo, *el* conocid**o** *muralista* Diego Rivera.

Actividad 1.17

This is the order in which the following questions appear in the recording.

1 ¿Cómo te llamas?

2 ¿Eres de aquí?

3 Y tu familia, ¿de dónde es?

4 ¿Cuánto tiempo hace que vives aquí?

5 ¿Cómo es Toledo?

6 ¿Por qué es tan famosa Toledo?

7 ¿Qué hay para visitar?

8 ¿Y hay muchos turistas en Toledo?

9 ¿De qué países son los turistas?

10 ¿Qué idiomas hablas?

11 ¿Cómo es la gente en Toledo?

Actividad 1.18

Here is a model answer:

1   Me llamo Dorothy Calderwood.

2   Soy de Inglaterra.

3   Hablo francés y un poco de alemán.

4   Mi familia es inglesa, de Liverpool.

5   Trabajo en la *Open University* de administradora.

Actividad 1.20

The hidden words are ringed in the box below:

e	b	u	s	e	y	l	a	i	r
b	a	t	a	h	t	u	k	c	a
c	r	o	ñ	u	c	o	f	e	b
s	o	j	o	n	a	e	g	o	r
a	v	e	s	t	i	d	o	i	a
b	e	r	o	i	b	u	r	t	b
e	u	j	n	a	s	a	d	i	i
g	a	r	t	a	l	t	o	d	l
b	i	o	f	s	e	a	r	i	t
n	s	a	c	e	p	i	t	o	f
u	g	a	l	e	b	u	r	a	k

Actividad 2.1

1   Antonio Martínez is from Soria, in the autonomous region of Castilla y León.

2   Begoña Iturriate is from the País Vasco. Bilbao is in the País Vasco and she says she speaks Basque.

3   Montse Fuente is from Cataluña. She speaks Catalan and is from the north-east of the peninsula.

4   Moncho Pardo is from Galicia. He lives in the north-west of Spain and speaks Galician.

5   Ana Almeida is from Andalucía. She was born in Seville and she says that, although she lives in Madrid, she has not lost her Andalusian accent.

Actividad 2.2

The eight verbs that describe what Teresa and Omar did are:

saludar	tomar (algo)	explicar	quedar
ir (a algún sitio)	preguntar	invitar	decir (adiós)

Actividad 2.3

Teresa could have described the events in her day as follows:

1   He ido a la Escuela Oficial de Idiomas con Omar.
    or   Omar y yo hemos ido a la Escuela Oficial de Idiomas.

2   He tomado un café.

3   He charlado con Omar en el bar.
    or   Omar y yo hemos charlado en el bar.

4   He dado clase.

Actividad 2.4

1   Falso (She says: 'Lo siento, sé que me he retrasado un poco.')

2   Falso (He says: 'No se disculpe, no hay ningún problema.')

3   Falso (He says: 'Buenos días… ' so he is being polite, not aggressive.)

4   Verdadero

5   Falso (She says: 'España es muy variada lingüísticamente… ')

6   Verdadero

7   Verdadero

8   Falso (She has to go because she is busy: 'Tengo que subir al despacho de los profesores y terminar de preparar mi clase de hoy.')

9   Verdadero

10 Verdadero

Actividad 2.5

Ser *(indicating characteristic features)*

Ser puntual	Ser variado lingüísticamente (un país)
Ser agresivo	Ser amable

Estar *(indicating mood)*

Estar enfadado	Estar interesado por (algo)
Estar confuso	Estar aburrido
Estar bien informado	Estar contento

Actividad 2.6

Here is the complete letter. The words you should have inserted are in bold.

Escuela Oficial de Idiomas
c/ Cisneros, 74
39007 Santander   8 de noviembre de 1998

Estimados señores:

Me dirijo a ustedes para pedirles información sobre sus cursos. **He estudiado** español durante cinco años y estoy muy interesada en la cultura de su país. **He visitado** España en varias ocasiones, pero sólo **he ido** de turista. Recientemente, mi jefe me **ha ofrecido** la posibilidad de trabajar en Madrid durante unos meses. Creo que **es** muy importante conocer la cultura del país para estar bien integrada. **He visto** en la Internet que ustedes ofrecen cursos de cultura española y **he pensado** que **son** ideales para mí. Les agradecería que me mandaran información sobre la matrícula.

Muchas gracias de antemano.

Atentamente,

D. Calderwood

Actividad 2.7

Ordenador / Computador / Computadora:

1	la pantalla	**2**	el módem
3	el ratón	**4**	el teclado
5	el cable	**6**	el altavoz
7	el disquete	**8**	el enchufe

Teléfono móvil:

9 el botón   **10** el auricular   **11** la antena

Buzón y carta:

12 el buzón   **13** el sobre

14 la dirección   **15** sello

Actividad 2.8

1 The subject of the report is the mobile phone (*teléfono móvil*).

2 (a) España, Francia, Gran Bretaña   (e)   Italia

(b) Italia   (f)   Gran Bretaña

(c) Alemania   (g)   Italia

(d) Estados Unidos

Actividad 2.9

There are various possibilities in each case.

1 El teléfono es **más** rápido **que** la carta.

El teléfono es **menos** económico **que** la carta.

La carta es **más** confidencial **que** el teléfono.

La carta es **más** económica **que** el teléfono.

La carta es **menos** rápida **que** el teléfono.

2 El correo electrónico es **tan** seguro **como** la carta.

El correo electrónico es **más** rápido **que** la carta.

La carta es **más** lenta **que** el correo electrónico.

3 El ordenador es **más** económico **que** el teléfono móvil.

El ordenador es **tan** moderno **como** el teléfono móvil.

El ordenador es **más** lento **que** el teléfono móvil.

Actividad 2.12

Some possible answers are given below:

El teléfono móvil no vale **para** recibir mensajes escritos.

El correo electrónico se usa **en** todo el mundo **para** enviar mensajes mediante un módem.

Las cartas son **para** comunicarse por escrito.

El teléfono es **para** comunicarse oralmente.

Hay teléfonos públicos **en** la calle.

Actividad 2.13

Here is the whole article. The words you should have provided are in bold.

> **S**e calcula que actualmente, más de 30 millones de internautas viajan virtualmente desde sus ordenadores **para** encontrar un tesoro: la información. **En** España existen más de 230.000 usuarios de la Internet y la mayoría de ellos la usan **para** fines científicos y académicos.
>
> Sin duda, la magia de esta red **para** el usuario español, igual que **para** el resto, se encuentra **en** los servicios que ofrece. Debido a la juventud del servicio **en** nuestro país, España actúa **en** la Internet como una esponja: 'estamos aquí **para** chupar información, no **para** ofrecerla', reconoce Juan Antonio Esteban, gerente del proveedor Goya.

(Adaptado de Jiménez, Marimar, «Internautas españoles» en *El País Dominical*)

Actividad 2.14

You should have ticked the boxes for **all** the activities.

(a) vaciar los buzones

(b) clasificar cartas

(c) empaquetar las cartas

(d) repartir el correo

(e) conducir la furgoneta de correos

(f) levantarse temprano

(g) trabajar por las tardes

(h) trabajar los fines de semana

(i) utilizar máquinas

Actividad 2.15

The correct answers are as follows:

1 Luis y Enrique usan un carrito para llevar las cartas.

2 Hay tantas mujeres como hombres en la profesión de cartero.

3 Las mujeres introdujeron el carrito para llevar las cartas.

4 Enrique escribe pocas cartas.

5 La novia de Enrique nunca responde a sus cartas.

Actividad 2.16

1 Here are the Spanish words for those items that are used in the recordings:

(a) postman   *cartero*

(b) mail   *correo / correspondencia*

(c) letters   *cartas*

(d) postbox   *buzón*

(e) van   *furgoneta*

(f) postal bag   *cartera*

(g) trolley / little trolley   *carro / carrito*

(h) postcards   *postales*

(i) fines, bills and court orders   *multas, facturas y cosas del Juzgado*

(j) I stop writing   *dejo de escribir*

2 This is one way of organizing the words in the mind-map:

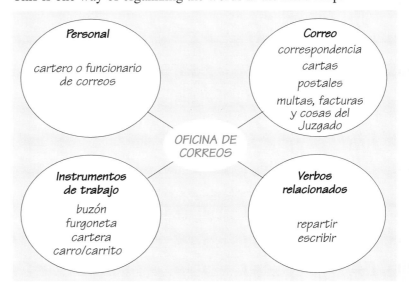

Actividad 2.17

Here are some examples of the kind of answer you might have given:

1 **Lo mejor de ser cartero** es no trabajar por las tardes.

2 **Lo peor de ser cartero** es levantarse muy temprano.
Lo peor de ser cartero es la monotonía.

3 **La mayor parte del correo** es oficial o propaganda.

4 **La menor parte del correo** son cartas personales.

5 **Es mejor** escribir cartas a los amigos. / Es mejor escribirles.
 Es mejor llamar por teléfono a los amigos. / Es mejor llamarles por teléfono.

Actividad 2.18

2 **Personal *a* (where direct object is named or specific):**

He visto **a un amigo**.

Hoy he visto dos veces **a tu padre**.

Escuchan atentamente **al profesor**.

¿Conocéis **a Miguel**?

Ana va a visitar **a sus abuelos**.

Teresa escribió **a su madre**.

Vi **a tu perro** corriendo por el jardín.

No personal *a* (where direct object denotes unidentified person or animal):

He visto **un hombre**.

Vi **un perro** corriendo por el jardín.

No personal *a* (where direct object is inanimate)

He visto dos veces **esa película**.

Siempre escuchan **la radio** por las tardes.

¿Conocéis **Toledo**?

Ana va a visitar **la catedral** de Toledo.

Teresa escribió **una carta** muy larga.

3 Here are some possible answers:

He recogido **a** los niños del colegio.

Miramos **a** Juan de arriba abajo.

Nunca oigo **a** mi padre cuando entra en casa.

¿Has visto mi libro por alguna parte?

Quieren visitar la judería de Toledo.

Conoce **a** Susana desde que era una niña.

Actividad 3.1

2 Your sentences might look something like the following:

Voy de compras con frecuencia.

Siempre limpio el coche.

Nunca arreglo el jardín.

A veces veo la tele.

Casi nunca voy al campo.

Voy al cine con frecuencia.

A veces visito a la familia.

Salgo a tomar una copa con frecuencia.

Salgo con los amigos con frecuencia.

Nunca estoy sin hacer nada.

A veces lavo la ropa.

Actividad 3.2

1 They are in a bar.

2 It is quite an intimate mood, judging from the conversation and the general atmosphere. But it also becomes quite sad when Omar talks about his divorce.

Actividad 3.3

1 (a) The following are some famous Spanish films, with their directors:

El espíritu de la colmena (Dir. Víctor Erice)

Belle époque (Dir. Fernando Trueba)

Tacones lejanos (Dir. Pedro Almodóvar)

Átame (Dir. Pedro Almodóvar)

Viridiana (Dir. Luis Buñuel)

El perro del hortelano (Dir. Pilar Miró)

Jamón, jamón (Dir. Bigas Luna)

(b) Famous Spanish actors and actresses include:

Maribel Verdú	Carmen Maura
Victoria Abril	Antonio Resines
Javier Bardem	Antonio Banderas
Fernando Rey	Fernando Fernán-Gómez

2 The key words for each film are shown in bold and the genres they belong to added:

La buena estrella. España 1997. Dir. Ricardo Franco. Un hombre mayor inicia una inesperada relación con una joven **huérfana**. El **ex novio** de la chica huérfana vuelve y se muda con la pareja: un triángulo amoroso nada convencional.

DRAMA

Memorias de ángel caído. España 1997. Los debutantes Fernando Cámara y David Alonso han empezado su carrera con una historia de **zombies** que vuelven a la vida después de ser **envenenados.**

TERROR

Hazlo por mí. España 1997. Dir. Ángel Fernández Santos. La seducción y la **manipulación** son las claves de esta historia. Un ejecutivo aburrido es arrastrado a un mundo de **delincuencia** por una irresistible mujer.

SUSPENSE

Gracias por la propina. España 1997. Dir. Francesc Bellmunt. La **infancia** y la **adolescencia** de dos niños huérfanos criados en la Valencia de los **años 60** se convierte en un **canto** a la tolerancia.

ROMÁNTICA

Actividad 3.4

1 Pepa: personaje principal de la película *Mujeres al borde de un ataque de nervios.*

(Pedro) Almodóvar: director de la misma película.

Carmen Maura: la actriz que desempeña el papel de Pepa.

Antonio Banderas: uno de los actores principales.

2 Film

Sesión

Película

Autorizada para todos los públicos

Cartelera

Premios Goya

Actividad 3.5

1 (a) Sí, le ha gustado mucho.

(b) Goya.

(c) Piensa que son muy trágicos.

2 Omar says:

Es impresionante,

and later:

Todo el museo es una maravilla.

He could also have said:

Es fenomenal,

and:

Todo el museo es estupendo.

Actividad 3.6

1 (a) Los museos.

(b) Estudiar.

(c) Vivir en Toledo (*she doesn't want to go and live there*).

2 Your answers might look like this:

(a) Me gustan los berberechos pero no me gustan las aceitunas.

(b) Me gusta bailar la salsa pero no me gusta bailar el rock.

(c) Me gusta la paella pero no me gustan los caracoles.

(d) Me gusta dormir la siesta pero no me gusta trabajar después de comer.

(e) Me gusta bañarme en la playa pero no me gusta bañarme en la piscina.

Actividad 3.8

1	**qu**eso	**5**	**c**uchillo	**9**	**c**uadrado
2	bal**c**ón	**6**	abani**c**o	**10**	**c**ruz
3	**k**imono *or* **qu**imono	**7**	**c**ráter	**11**	**Qu**ijote
4	cha**qu**eta	**8**	bar**c**o	**12**	**c**orazón

The rules you should have worked out for spelling the sound /k/ are:

1 *qu* is used before *e* and *i*;

2 *c* is used before the other vowels and all consonants;

3 *k* is rarely used in Spanish, except for foreign words, and weights and measures (*kilo, kilómetro*).

Actividad 3.9

1 The restaurants you might have chosen, according to the preferences suggested, are:

Bola Taverna, because it offers the *cocido madrileño*; or **La Plaza de Chamberí** or **Café Gijón**, because they are in your price range and have a pavement area.

Posada de la Villa is a bit too expensive for your budget.

Casa Alberto seems to specialize in fish, which you don't like, and seafood.

La Pampa is not typical of Madrid.

2 You may have matched the questions and answers as follows:

(a) ¿Por qué no vamos al 'Café Gijón'?

(iii) Lo siento, no me apetece.

(b) ¿Te apetece ir a 'Casa Alberto'?

(i) Sí, claro, parece que está muy bien de precio.

(c) ¿Te apetece un restaurante argentino?

(ii) No, me gustaría algo típico madrileño.

(d) ¿Quieres ir al restaurante 'Posada de la Villa'?

(vi) Quizás, pero, ¿no es un poco caro?

(e) ¿Te gustaría ir a la 'Bola Taverna'?

(iv) ¡Cómo no! ¡Me encantaría probar el cocido madrileño!

(f) ¿Te apetecería ir a 'La Plaza de Chamberí'?

(v) ¡Estupendo! ¿Tiene aparcamiento?

Actividad 3.10

1 There are different possibilities. Here is one model:

	Tiempo	Actividad
Soria	lluvia	visitar un museo, quedarse en el hotel leyendo
San Sebastián	viento	pescar, hacer volar la cometa, hacer windsurf
Sierra de Guadarrama	nubes y claros	salir a pasear, jugar al tenis, hacer montañismo, ir de excursión, pescar
Cuenca	despejado (sol)	ir a un restaurante con terraza, pescar, tomar el sol, bañarse, tomar un helado, salir a pasear, jugar al tenis

2 Your answer might look something like this:

> En primavera hace buen tiempo, pero en verano no hace mucho sol. En otoño llueve mucho y hace viento. En invierno siempre nieva.

Actividad 3.12

1 La actividad de tiempo libre más popular en España es **ver la televisión**.

2 Your answers could look like this:

(a) Escuchar música.

(b) Mis hobbies preferidos son: pasear, ir al cine y escuchar música.

(c) Las actividades que no practico son: ir a bailar, hacer trabajos manuales e ir a espectáculos musicales.

Actividad 3.13

1–3 Here is what Spaniards in general like doing in their spare time, and what Juan would like to do if he had more time:

Los españoles	Juan
salir por la noche	hacer deporte
beber en los bares	jugar al fútbol
bailar	salir por la noche
pasárselo bien	conocer gente
salir por la calle	conocer chicas
estar con otras personas	
charlar	

Actividad 3.14

This is what Juan says about each of these occasions:

Una fiesta con amigos

Llevamos una botella de algo, o algo para picar.

Me gusta reírme.

Me gusta charlar con la gente.

Me gusta contar chistes.

Me gusta contar anécdotas del día.

Me gusta hablar de mujeres.

Hablamos de cualquier cosa menos de trabajo.

187

Un cumpleaños en el pueblo con familiares y amigos

Nos reunimos allí con una tarta.

Mi madre nos atiende a todos.

Nos sentimos muy felices.

Me tiran de las orejas.

Me dan regalos pequeños.

Actividad 3.15

Your description might look like this:

> Los señores cerca de la barra **están charlando**. Uno de ellos **está contando** una historia y los otros **están escuchando**. Uno de los hombres **está bebiendo** algo. El camarero **está limpiando** un vaso. Cerca de la puerta hay un señor que **está pintando** un cuadro.

Actividad 3.16

Crossword:

- 1 Down: PARAGUAS
- 2 Down: DICIEMBRE
- 3 Across: PRIMAVERA
- 4 Down: MEDIODÍA
- 5 Across: VACACIONES
- 6 Down: AGENDA
- 7 Down: MES
- 8 Across: BAUTISMO
- 9 Down: JUNIO
- 10 Across: LLUVIA
- 11 Across: RELOJ

Actividad 4.1

1 Teresa phones her mother.

2 Yes, until she hears that Omar is coming as well.

3 No. She didn't even know of his existence.

4 At the railway station.

Actividad 4.2

Here are some possible ways of asking the questions:

1 ¿Cuándo va Teresa a Toledo?

2 ¿Quién va a Toledo con Teresa? / ¿Con quién va Teresa a Toledo?

3 ¿De dónde es Omar?

4 ¿A qué hora sale el tren para Toledo?

5 ¿Por qué compran billete de ida y vuelta?

6 ¿Cuánto dura el viaje de Madrid a Toledo?

Actividad 4.3

1 **What?**	**Who?**
... voy a verte este fin de semana.	Teresa
¿Vas a traerme a otra de tus tontas amigas?	Doña Amelia
¿Es que vas a casarte?	Doña Amelia
... mañana voy a ir a verte...	Teresa
... voy a ir con él.	Teresa
Y ahora voy a cortar (el teléfono).	Teresa

2 Your sentences might look like this:

Este fin de semana voy a visitar a una amiga en otra ciudad.

El sábado por la tarde vamos a ir a pasear por el campo.

El domingo por la mañana vamos a ir a la piscina cerca de su casa.

El domingo por la tarde voy a volver a mi casa.

El domingo por la noche voy a quedarme en casa.

Actividad 4.4

1	Teresa y Omar van temprano a la estación.	**Verdadero**	
2	Los trenes de Madrid a Toledo no salen con mucha regularidad.	**Falso**	('Hay un tren cada hora.')
3	Teresa y Omar ya tienen sus billetes.	**Falso**	('Podemos ir ya a comprar los billetes, si te parece.')
4	Los billetes de ida y vuelta resultan más baratos.	**Verdadero**	
5	El viaje de Madrid a Toledo dura tres horas.	**Falso**	('Tras una hora de viaje, Teresa y Omar llegan a la estación de Toledo.')
6	La madre de Teresa vive cerca de la estación.	**Verdadero**	
7	Omar y Teresa se van a dar un paseo.	**Falso**	('Podemos dar un paseo…' 'No, espera, seguro que está.')
8	Teresa cree que su madre no está en casa.	**Falso**	('No, espera, seguro que está. Ella sabe que vamos a venir.')

Actividad 4.5

You probably found this activity quite difficult. It takes a fair amount of practice to fine-tune your ear to the different intonation patterns.

Here are the questions you will have heard in this part of the cassette, with the corresponding intonation. The rising or falling syllables are underlined.

— ¿<u>Sí</u>, dí<u>game</u>?   ↑ ↑

— ¿Ma<u>má</u>?   ↑

— ¿Eres <u>tú</u>, Te<u>re</u>sa?   ↑ ↑

— ¿Cómo es<u>tás</u>?   ↓

— ¿Cuándo vi<u>enes</u>?   ↓

— ¿Viene tam<u>bién</u>, Car<u>men</u>?   ↑ ↑

— ¿Vas a traerme a otra de tus tontas a<u>migas</u>?   ↑

— ¿Un <u>hom</u>bre?   ↑

— ¿No<u>vio</u>?   ↑

Actividad 4.6

1 (a) Voy a leer en la playa.

   (b) Vamos a jugar a la pelota.

   (c) Vamos a hacer turismo.

   (d) Voy a hacer / tomar / sacar fotos.

Actividad 4.7

1 (a) Carmen.

   (b) No, no es muy caro.

   (c) El veintidós de febrero.

   (d) A las 3 de la mañana (hora de aquí).

2 (a) Teresa y Doña Amelia no **van a** viajar a México.

   (b) El vuelo **va a** ser muy largo.

   (c) ¿Qué día **van a** volar a México Carmen y Mercedes?

   (d) ¿Cuánto **va a** costar?

   (e) Yo no **voy a** ir a México.

Actividad 4.9

Here is the complete text. The missing prepositions are indicated in bold.

> Este año, Carmen va a ir **a** México de vacaciones **por** dos semanas.
> No va sola: va **con** su tía. Siempre ha querido ir a México. Su avión
> sale **de** Madrid y no hace escala en ninguna parte. Vuela directo
> **hasta/a** México. Allí Carmen y su tía Mercedes van a alojarse **en** un
> hotel **por** cinco días. Han alquilado un coche y van a viajar **por** todo
> el país, así que **hasta** el día que tienen que regresar **a** España, van a
> visitar los lugares que Carmen siempre ha deseado conocer.

Actividad 4.10

Here are different ways of describing what Carmen has to do:

12 de julio

Va a acabar el trabajo a las doce. / A las doce va a acabar el trabajo.

Va a comer con Elisa en el Restaurante Neptuno a la una y media. / A la una y media va a comer con Elisa en el Restaurante Neptuno.

Va a recoger los billetes a la agencia de viajes a las cuatro y media. / A las cuatro y media va a recoger los billetes a la agencia de viajes.

Va a recoger a Teresa a la Escuela Oficial de Idiomas a las cinco y cuarto. / A las cinco y cuarto va a recoger a Teresa a la Escuela Oficial de Idiomas.

13 de julio

Por la mañana va a ir al banco a recoger los cheques de viaje. / Va a ir al banco a recoger los cheques de viaje por la mañana.

También va a ir a comprar bronceador y otras cosillas a la droguería.

A las doce y media va a ir al hospital con Mercedes (a ponerse la última inyección). / Va a ir al hospital con Mercedes a las doce y media.

Por la tarde va a comprar un bañador nuevo y va a hacer las maletas. / Va a comprar un bañador nuevo y va a hacer las maletas por la tarde.

Actividad 4.11

2   This is how the words are spelt:

coger	viajar	pasaje
ojo	caja	genio
jarabe	geranio	julio
girar	ginebra	mojado
reloj	régimen	pelirrojo

Actividad 4.12

These are names that correspond to the things you see at the airport:

(a) monitor

(b) mostrador de facturación

(c) maleta

(d) pasajero

(e) carrito

(f) control de seguridad

(g) cinta transportadora de equipajes

(h) Llegadas

(i) Salidas

(j) tienda libre de impuestos

Actividad 4.13

1 Here are some questions that you might ask people waiting for a flight:

¿A qué hora sale su vuelo?

¿Por qué puerta sale el vuelo?

¿Viaja solo(, -a) o acompañado(, -a)?

¿Va de vacaciones o viaja por negocios?

¿Lleva mucho equipaje?

2 This is how you should have answered:

	Carlos	María Elena
Viaja al continente americano.	✓	✓
Sabe por qué puerta sale su vuelo.		
Hace escala en Europa.	✓	
Viaja solo(, -a).		
Viaja por negocios.	✓	
Le gusta leer en el avión.	✓	
Lleva dos maletas.	✓	
Viaja con su hijo.		✓
Ha viajado por todo el mundo.	✓	
Su vuelo tarda ocho horas.		✓

Actividad 4.14

(a) la duración del vuelo   (v) cinco, seis horas

(b) el motivo de su viaje   (iii) negocios

(c) lo que le gusta hacer en el avión   (x) leer

(d) los ha visitado   (ii) más de cincuenta países

(e) el lugar de la escala   (vi) París

(f) los medios de transporte   (xi) globo aerostático y
que no ha utilizado   submarino

(g) las personas con quienes viaja   (vii) compañeros de trabajo

(h) la duración de su estancia   (viii) tres o cuatro semanas

(i) su equipaje   (ix) dos maletas

(j) la hora de salida de su vuelo   (iv) a la una, más o menos

(k) el destino de su vuelo   (i) Toronto

Actividad 4.15

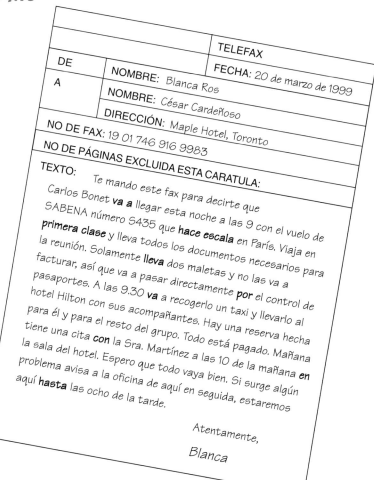

TELEFAX

FECHA: 20 de marzo de 1999

DE — NOMBRE: Blanca Ros

A — NOMBRE: César Cardeñoso

DIRECCIÓN: Maple Hotel, Toronto

NO DE FAX: 19 01 746 916 9983

NO DE PÁGINAS EXCLUIDA ESTA CARATULA:

TEXTO: Te mando este fax para decirte que Carlos Bonet **va a** llegar esta noche a las 9 con el vuelo de SABENA número S435 que **hace escala** en París. Viaja en **primera clase** y lleva todos los documentos necesarios para la reunión. Solamente **lleva** dos maletas y no las va a facturar, así que va a pasar directamente **por** el control de pasaportes. A las 9.30 **va** a recogerlo un taxi y llevarlo al hotel Hilton con sus acompañantes. Hay una reserva hecha para él y para el resto del grupo. Todo está pagado. Mañana tiene una cita **con** la Sra. Martínez a las 10 de la mañana **en** la sala del hotel. Espero que todo vaya bien. Si surge algún problema avisa a la oficina de aquí en seguida, estaremos aquí **hasta** las ocho de la tarde.

Atentamente,

Blanca

Actividad 4.16

According to the cassette:

1   María Elena and her husband are travelling with their son as well.

2   They have four suitcases.

3   They are leaving at 14.55.

Actividad 4.17

1	La mujer viaja mucho por Europa.	**Falso**	(La mujer viaja mucho por Centroamérica.)
2	Su avión sale a las tres menos cinco.	**Verdadero**	
3	La mujer no sabe a qué hora sale su avión.	**Falso**	(La mujer no sabe por qué puerta sale su vuelo.)
4	Su vuelo tarda más o menos nueve horas.	**Falso**	(Su vuelo tarda aproximadamente ocho horas.)
5	Su vuelo hace dos escalas: en Miami y El Salvador.	**Falso**	(Su vuelo hace una escala, en Miami.)
6	La mujer viaja sólo con su hijo.	**Falso**	(La mujer viaja con su marido y su hijo.)
7	No lleva mucho equipaje.	**Verdadero**	
8	La mujer trata de mantener a su hijo despierto durante el vuelo.	**Falso**	(La mujer trata de dormir a su hijo durante el vuelo.)

Actividad 4.18

1   The columns below show the person to whom the following sentences apply:

(a) … has four pieces of luggage.	María Elena
(b) … is on a business trip.	Carlos
(c) … is travelling with his/her family.	María Elena
(d) … says that s/he has never been on a submarine.	Carlos
(e) … has visited over fifty countries.	Carlos
(f) … is on a flight with a stopover in America.	María Elena
(g) … is going to be flying for eight hours.	María Elena

2   The negative sentences should read as follows:

(a) Carlos no tiene cuatro maletas.

(b) María Elena no viaja por negocios.

(c) Carlos no viaja con su familia.

(d) María Elena no dice que nunca ha viajado en submarino.

(e) María Elena no ha visitado más de cincuenta países.

(f) Carlos no va a hacer escala en Miami.

(g) Carlos no va a volar durante ocho horas.

Actividad 4.19

This is how you should have divided up the words:

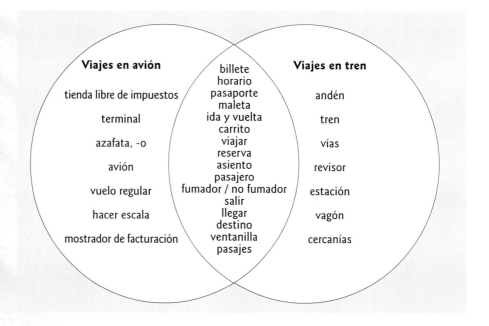

Actividad 5.1

1 The sketch below shows where you are likely to find the appropriate objects in a Spanish house:

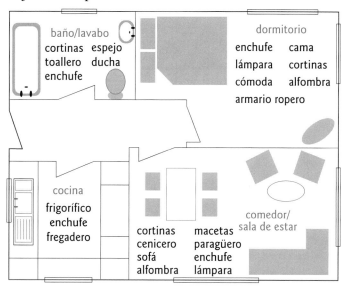

El semáforo (traffic lights), *el puerto* (port) and *el escaparate* (shop window) are not related to the theme of the home.

2 Other related words are:

almohada (la)	bañera (la)	buhardilla (la)	colcha (la)
cuadro (el)	despacho (el)	ducha (la)	estudio (el)
escalera (la)	escritorio (el)	estantería (la)	garaje (el)
lavadora (la)	lavaplatos (el)	manta (la)	mesa (la)
mesilla (de noche) (la)	nevera (la)	pared (la)	pasillo (el)
patio (el)	persiana (la)	piso (el)	planta (la)
recibidor (el)	sábanas (las)	salón (el)	silla (la)
sillón (el)	sótano (el)	suelo (el)	techo (el)
terraza (la)	toalla (la)	ventana (la)	

Actividad 5.2

1	La madre y Omar se besan.	**Falso**	(No, ella sólo le dice 'hola'.)
2	La madre se va al baño.	**Falso**	(No, se va a la cocina.)
3	Teresa y Omar se sientan a hablar.	**Falso**	(No, visitan la casa.)
4	A Omar le gusta la casa.	**Verdadero**	

Actividad 5.3

Picture (a) matches the description:

Los tres se dirigen al salón.

El salón es grande, pero con pocos muebles. En el centro hay un sofá de piel y una gran butaca enfrente. Al fondo hay una chimenea y un reloj muy antiguo. De las paredes cuelgan cuadros con retratos de familiares. Las ventanas son estrechas y dan poca luz. La madre de Teresa se dirige a su butaca e invita a Omar a que se siente.

Actividad 5.4

1 This is what the following abbreviations mean:

coc.	cocina	tlf.	teléfono
calefacc.	calefacción	apto.	apartamento
hab.	habitación	p. baja	planta baja
tza.	terraza		
z.	zona		

2 The flat you should have chosen is (c). It is suitable because:

it is in a central area *(cerca centro);*
it is less than 100,000 pesetas per month *(70.000 mes);*
it has 2 bedrooms *(dos dormitorios);*
it has a bathroom *(baño).*

(a) is not suitable because it consists of only one room *(se alquila hab.).*

(b) is not suitable because it has no lift and is on the top floor *(bonito ático).*

(d) is not suitable because it is on the outskirts *(situado en las afueras).*

Actividad 5.5

This is how you should have matched the words:

unas ventanas anchas y blancas   un sillón blando y limpio

un comedor limpio   una habitación oscura

unas lámparas apagadas,   unas cortinas blancas y anchas
blancas y anchas

Actividad 5.8

1 Here is the suggested advice to Omar in complete sentences:

(a) Entra por la ventana.

(b) Ve al supermercado.

(c) Pon la calefacción.

(d) Pon la lavadora.

(e) Busca en la cómoda.

(f) Pasa el trapo del polvo.

(g) Entra la colada.

(h) Ve más temprano.

2 Below are some answers you might have given:

(a) Usa productos naturales.

(b) Compra comida sin envoltorio.

(c) Apaga las luces si no las usas.

(d) Recicla la basura.

(e) Limpia con vinagre, jabón o limón.

(f) Dúchate para gastar menos agua.

(g) Rodéate de plantas en tu casa.

Actividad 5.9

Here is the complete text with the correct answers in bold:

> El despacho de mi padre era amplio y confortable. Tenía un escritorio, y **detrás** del escritorio, un sillón. **Delante** había dos sillas para las visitas. **A la derecha** había dos sillones, y **entre** los sillones, una lámpara. **Encima de / Sobre** la mesa tenía siempre muchos papeles y también una lámpara **a la derecha / encima**. También había un teléfono **a la izquierda**. A la izquierda del escritorio tenía una mesa y **sobre** ella, la máquina de escribir.

Al fondo del despacho había una ventana, **entre** dos grandes estanterías con libros.

En el suelo, **debajo** del escritorio, había una gran alfombra.

Actividad 5.10

2 Here are the correct answers:

(a) Vive en una casa unifamiliar. **Verdadero**

(b) Es una casa pequeña, pero muy bonita. **Verdadero**

(c) Tiene portería. **Falso** (No, tiene portero automático.)

(d) Vive en un edificio de dos pisos. **Verdadero**

Actividad 5.11

1 Falso ('… es una casa típica toledana.')

2 Verdadero

3 Verdadero

4 Verdadero

5 Falso ('Pues es una decoración muy sencilla porque este tipo de viviendas son unas viviendas populares con muy pocas manifestaciones externas de riqueza.')

Actividad 5.12

2 Your letter might look like this:

Estimado señor/señora:

Me gustaría intercambiar mi casa con alguien en España con una casa similar durante el mes de agosto. Yo tengo una casa con dos plantas. Es una casa muy céntrica. Los comercios están a menos de cinco minutos andando. Tiene tres habitaciones en el piso de arriba y un baño. En el piso de abajo hay una cocina, un estudio y el salón comedor. No tiene balcones ni terraza pero tiene un jardín en la parte trasera. Toda la casa es exterior.

Si está interesado/a, escriba a Christine Maguire, 29, Lochrin Buildings, Tollcross, Edinburgh, Scotland.

Atentamente,

C. Maguire

Actividad 5.13

2 Here are some model sentences:

(a) (*sheet*) Dame dos **hojas** de papel.
(*leaf*) En otoño el parque está lleno de las **hojas** de los árboles.

(b) (*quarter*) El **casco** antiguo de Valencia es muy bonito.
(*helmet*) Los militares de las Naciones Unidas llevan **cascos** azules.

(c) (*storey*) La oficina de marketing está en el último **piso**.
(*floor*) Voy a limpiar el **piso**, está muy sucio.

Actividad 5.14

1 *Persiana* does not refer to household linen or soft furnishing.

2 *Cuarto* does not refer to a type of house.

3 *Mesa* does not refer to a part of a building.

4 *Cuadro* does not refer to a specific room.

5 *Comedor* does not refer to a piece of furniture.

Actividad 6.1

2 This is what you should have found out in Episode 6:

(a) (ii) Teresa y Omar están disgustados.

(b) (ii) Teresa y Omar se quedan un rato más en Toledo.

(c) (ii) Teresa explica a Omar la razón de la actitud de su madre.

(d) (ii) Teresa y Omar deciden casarse.

Actividad 6.2

To offer drinks	*¿Qué quieres tomar?*
To offer food	*¿Qué quieres comer?*
To attract attention	*¿Camarero, por favor?*
To order drinks	*Yo quiero un zumo de naranja. / … y yo una tónica.*
To order food	*Patatas bravas, gracias.*

Actividad 6.3

This is the correct sequence of events:

2 Teresa se quedó embarazada.

6 Fue una noche tonta, una equivocación.

5 El padre de Carmen tenía miedo.

3 La familia del padre de Carmen dio algo de dinero.

1 La familia del padre de Carmen se marchó al extranjero.

4 Doña Amelia se quedó viuda.

Actividad 6.4

1 Words used in the Audio Drama referring to relationships are given below, together with the person they apply to:

	Omar	**Teresa**	**Doña Amelia**
Salir juntos			
Boda			
Querer a alguien		✓	
Enamorarse			
Casarse		✓	
Quedarse viuda			✓
Dejar a alguien			
(Tener) relaciones		✓	
Quedarse embarazada		✓	
Engañar a alguien			

2

Expresión	**Uso**	**Con referencia a…**
querer a alguien	'¿Pero no te quería?'	Teresa's former boyfriend (Carmen's father)
casarse	'No nos casamos porque sus padres no querían.'/ '¡Y menos mal que no nos casamos!'	Teresa and her former boyfriend
quedarse viuda/o	'Bueno, pues ella ya era viuda.'	Doña Amelia
(tener) relaciones	'Desde entonces, (ella) no quiere saber nada de mis relaciones con hombres.'	Teresa's relationships with men
quedarse embarazada	'Desde que me quedé embarazada, está igual conmigo.'	Teresa

Actividad 6.5

While the lists you make will depend on your own views, older people may attach greater importance to such things as formal engagements and church weddings.

Actividad 6.6

1 The list of ingredients would include:
ensalada, jamón, tomate, calamares, pan, patatas, lomo, pimientos verdes, cangrejo, jamón de York, lechuga, salsa rosa, carne, salsa picante.

2 Here are a few possibilities:

Mi bocadillo favorito es el 'vegetal' porque me gusta la ensalada.

Mi bocadillo favorito es el 'malagueño' porque me gusta el jamón de York.

Mi bocadillo favorito es el 'campero' porque me gustan las patatas.

Mi bocadillo favorito es el 'mexicano' porque me gusta el picante.

Actividad 6.7

1 The pronominal verbs mentioned are *me levanto, me tomo* and *me acuesto*.

3 The two activities that Omar does and Teresa doesn't do are *coger el autobús* and *ver la televisión*.

Actividad 6.8

This is a model of what you might have answered:

Me levanto a las seis y media.

Desayuno a las siete.

Salgo de casa a las ocho.

Empiezo a trabajar a las nueve.

Termino de trabajar a las cinco.

Por la noche leo un libro.

Me acuesto a las once de la noche.

Actividad 6.9

1 El deporte más popular en Europa es el fútbol.

2 (Los países donde se come, fuma y bebe más son) Grecia, Portugal e Irlanda.

3 España.

4 La televisión.

5 En Inglaterra.

Actividad 6.10

Tongue-twisters are good mnemonics, as well as providing good practice in pronouncing difficult sounds. They are also great fun!

You will find more feedback on the cassette.

Actividad 6.11

2 En España…

    (a) … la comida principal es la del mediodía.   **Verdadero**

    (b) … el desayuno no es muy importante.   **Verdadero**

    (c) … la comida es un acto social.   **Verdadero**

    (d) … no es normal comer en familia.   **Falso**

    (e) … los niños generalmente cenan a media tarde.   **Falso**

Actividad 6.12

Sustantivo	Verbo	Verbo	Sustantivo
cena	**cenar**	comer	**comida**
merienda	**merendar**	desayunar	**desayuno**
bebida	**beber**	almorzar	**almuerzo**

If you were not sure how to complete the table, go on to the next *Curiosidad*, where you will find more information about Spanish eating habits.

Actividad 6.13

1 Here are the instructions for making a Spanish omelette, in the right order:

Pelar y lavar las patatas.	(4)
Pelar la cebolla.	(12)
Cortar las patatas y la cebolla en trozos pequeños.	(6)
Llenar la sartén de aceite hasta la mitad y calentar.	(9)
Freír las patatas y la cebolla.	(1)
Batir los huevos.	(8)
Añadir las patatas y la cebolla a los huevos batidos.	(2)
Echar sal al gusto.	(5)
Quitar el aceite sobrante de la sartén.	(11)
Echar todo a la sartén y freír.	(7)
Dar la vuelta con un plato o tapadera.	(10)
Hacer por el otro lado la tortilla.	(3)

2 Here is the whole recipe written with the impersonal *se* form:

> Primero se pelan y se lavan las patatas y la cebolla. Después se cortan las patatas y la cebolla en trozos pequeños. Luego se llena la sartén de aceite hasta la mitad y se calienta. Entonces se fríen las patatas y la cebolla. Se baten los huevos y, cuando estén listas, se añaden las patatas y la cebolla a los huevos batidos. Se echa sal al gusto. Luego se quita el aceite sobrante de la sartén, se echa todo a la sartén y se fríe. Entonces se da la vuelta con un plato o tapadera y finalmente se hace por el otro lado la tortilla.

Note that (like 'then' and 'next') *luego* and *después* are interchangeable. They can be used at any intermediate stage in the process to signal continuity.

Actividad 6.14

Here is the complete recipe with the answers in bold:

> Primero, **se lava** la almendra. Después **se mezcla** la almendra con los azúcares. **Se muele** la masa, **se tritura**, **se da** dos pasadas y luego **se le va** dando diferentes formas y **se le va** dando distintos rellenos.

Actividad 6.15

1 The fruit and vegetables match the descriptions as below:

(a) un cítrico redondo y anaranjado   (v)   naranja

(b) una verdura larga y anaranjada   (vii) zanahoria

(c) una fruta roja, amarilla o verde por fuera
y blanca por dentro   (x)   manzana

(d) una verdura de hojas verdes y blancas que
se usa en ensaladas   (iii) lechuga

(e) una fruta larga y amarilla   (ix) plátano

(f) una verdura redondeada con el centro blando,
recubierta de pequeñas hojas verdes   (xii) alcachofa

(g) una fruta tropical, amarilla por dentro
y marrón por fuera   (xi) piña

(h) parecen paraguas   (vi) champiñones

(i) una hortaliza marrón por fuera y blanca
por dentro   (i)   patatas

(j) es roja por fuera y por dentro, y se come
con ensaladas y con espaguettis   (viii) tomate

(k) tiene capas concéntricas por dentro y hace llorar   (iv) cebolla

(l) una hortaliza larga, verde por fuera y blanca
por dentro   (ii) pepino

2 Your descriptions might look like this:

(a) Rhubarb (*ruibarbo*): es una planta roja y verde con hojas largas: se come cocida y endulzada con helado y en tartas.

(b) Fennel (*hinojo*): es una planta verde y aromática con flores amarillas y hojas pequeñas que se usa en ensaladas y cocidos. A veces, también se usa para hacer té.

(c) Celery (*apio*): es una planta verde y alargada con troncos largos que se usa en sopas, ensaladas y sandwiches.

Actividad 6.16

1 En un mercado.

2 Lechugas, alcachofas, patatas, zanahorias, cebolletas.

3 Las patatas cuestan 175 pesetas; las zanahorias cuestan 75 pesetas; las lechugas cuestan 85 pesetas; las cebolletas cuestan 150 pesetas; las alcachofas cuestan 115 pesetas (el medio kilo).

4 La señora piensa que son muy caras.

Actividad 6.17

Opposite is a model of what a vegetarian, for example, might have chosen.

Actividad 7.1

1 This is how you should have matched the words and expressions:

caro	*expensive*	probar	*to try on*
barato	*cheap*	escaparate	*shop window*
cambio	*change*	pagar a plazos	*to pay in instalments*
rebajas	*sales*	recibo	*receipt*
talla	*size*	regatear	*to bargain*

2 This is how you should have answered:

(a) En unos grandes almacenes.

(b) Un vestido de boda.

(c) Dos.

(d) Color crema.

(e) Sesenta mil pesetas.

Verduras y hortalizas		**Frutas**		**Condimentos**	
judías verdes	☑	naranjas	☑	mostaza	☑
guisantes	☐	peras	☐	mahonesa	☐
tomates	☐	manzanas	☑	aceite	☐
patatas	☐	melón	☐	vinagre	☐
cebollas	☐	melocotones	☐	sal	☐
pimientos	☐	higos	☐	**Dulces**	
ajo	☑	uvas	☐	galletas	☐
calabacín	☐	nectarinas	☐	magdalenas	☐
berenjena	☑	**Legumbres**		mermelada	☐
col	☐	habas	☐	chocolate	☑
lechuga	☐	judías	☐	miel	☑
apio	☐	garbanzos	☑	**Productos lácteos y huevos**	
nabo	☐	guisantes	☐		
brécol	☐	lentejas	☐	huevos	☑
hinojo	☑	**Pescados**		queso	☑
Carnes		merluza	☐	yogur	☐
vaca	☐	bacalao	☐	leche	☐
cerdo	☐	trucha	☐	mantequilla	☐
cordero	☐	calamar	☐	margarina	☑
pollo	☐	**Bebidas**		**Cereales**	
Fiambres		agua mineral	☑	harina blanca	☐
jamón de York	☐	zumo	☑	harina integral	☑
jamón serrano	☐	vino tinto	☑	arroz blanco	☐
chorizo	☐	vino blanco	☐	arroz integral	☑
salmón ahumado	☐			maíz	☐

Actividad 7.2

Here are some possible questions:

¿Tienen una talla más pequeña?

¿Qué tallas tienen?

¿Cuánto cuesta esta falda?

¿Cuánto cuesta el pantalón?

¿Me puedo probar el abrigo?

¿Dónde puedo probarme el vestido?

Actividad 7.3

1   These are the opinions that Omar expresses:

(a) La verdad es que es bonito.

(b) Cuando te lo pongas, ya veré.

(c) Creo que no te va mucho.

(d) Me gusta.

(e) Realmente te sienta muy bien.

2   Your answer might look like this:

(a) Son bonitos pero están un poco pasados de moda.

(b) Creo que no es mi estilo. / Este estilo es bastante deportivo.

(c) La verdad es que son demasiado clásicos.

(d) Me gustan. / Son bonitos.

(e) Son un poco chillones, ¿no?

Actividad 7.4

2   (b) Teresa recibe una llamada en su teléfono móvil.

Actividad 7.5

These are the attitudes that the quotations reveal:

¿Para tu boda?	(surprise)
¿Ah sí?	(interest)
¿Sigues enfadada?	(reconciliation)
¡Mamá, estoy harta de que te metas en mi vida!	(anger)
¡No hagas esa locura, Teresa!	(warning)
¡Teresa! ¿Qué pasa?	(fear / anxiety)

Actividad 7.6

Here is what you can buy in each of these shops:

Ferretería: clavos, destornillador

Mercería: hilo de coser, botones

Farmacia: tiritas, jarabe

Librería: revistas, periódicos

Estanco: tabaco, sellos

Carnicería: longaniza, chuletas

Actividad 7.7

This is what the shopping lists should look like:

La lista de Omar

una bufanda
unos guantes de cuero
un jersey
unos pantalones de pana
un gorro de lana
unos calcetines de algodón
unas botas

un bañador
unas gafas de sol
un sombrero de paja
unas sandalias
una camiseta de algodón
unos pantalones cortos
un parasol
crema solar
una minifalda

La lista de Teresa

Actividad 7.8

This is what you should have written:

Las sandalias valen siete mil cuatrocientas pesetas.

La comida vale cinco mil doscientas noventa pesetas.

El vestido de novia vale sesenta mil pesetas.

Las gafas de sol valen doce mil novecientas pesetas.

La crema solar vale ochocientas veinticinco pesetas.

Actividad 7.9

Personal (subject) pronouns	Personal (direct object) pronouns
yo	me
tú	te
él/ella/Ud.	**lo/la**
nosotros, -as	nos
vosotros, -as	**os**
ellos/ellas/Uds.	**los/las**

Actividad 7.12

1   This is what your notes might look like:

Ha llamado	Jorge Julián	Pronovias	Una amiga
Mensaje	Quiere concertar una visita a domicilio para presentar la nueva Enciclopedia natural	¿A qué hora pueden traer el vestido de novia?	Va a ir al rastro a comprar una chaqueta de cuiro
Teléfono de contacto	355 47 70	Volverán a llamar	Llama más tarde

Actividad 7.13

This is how you should have matched the descriptions with the different kinds of shops:

Mercado

Es una gran extensión cubierta. Es un puesto de venta permanente. Tiene tiendas en su interior. Se pueden encontrar puestos de venta de diversos objetos.

Mercadillo

Venden objetos de segunda mano. Se celebra un día a la semana. Está al aire libre, en plazas y calles. Se pueden encontrar puestos de venta de diversos objetos.

Supermercado

Es una gran extensión cubierta. En él venden marcas comerciales conocidas. Es un puesto de venta permanente.

Actividad 7.14

These are the items that the person in the market wants to buy:

un jarrón

unos fruteros

unos juegos para consomé

Actividad 7.15

These are the prices, and the items they refer to:

500 pesetas

700 pesetas

un frutero

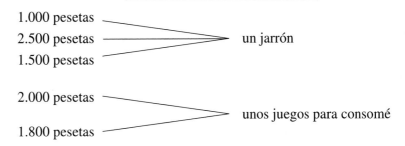

A bordo

1.000 pesetas

2.500 pesetas ——————→ un jarrón

1.500 pesetas

2.000 pesetas

——————→ unos juegos para consomé

1.800 pesetas

Actividad 7.16

Here is the whole transcript with the demonstratives in bold:

Cliente ¡Hola! ¿Me puedes enseñar **aquel** jarrón?

Vendedor ¿Cuál? ¿**Éste**?

Cliente Sí, el azul.

Vendedor El azul… ¡Mira! ¿Te gusta **ése**?

Cliente A lo mejor es un poco grande. ¿Tienes uno un poco más pequeño?

Vendedor Mira, tengo **éste** que es un poquito más pequeño. Mira a ver si te gusta **éste**.

Cliente **Éste** sí, me gusta más.

Vendedor ¿Te gusta más que el otro? Es algo más económico que el otro.

Cliente ¿Sale más barato?

Vendedor Sale más barato, sí.

Cliente ¡Ah, pues, me parece bien!

Vendedor Luego tienes también **ésos** de ahí… también azul.

Cliente ¡Ah, **ése** también me gusta! Y aparte de jarrón, ¿tienes platos, fruteros?

Vendedor Fruteros tienes **ésos** de ahí que tienes en el suelo…

Cliente Son de cerámica, ¿no?

Vendedor Sí, todos son de cerámica.

Cliente ¿Son de algún tipo de cerámica? ¿De Talavera o de Puente de Arzobispo?

Vendedor Es cerámica de Córdoba.

Cliente De Córdoba. ¿Qué precio tiene por ejemplo **éste**?

Vendedor **Ésos** a quinientas. **Este** otro a setecientas.

Cliente ¿Y el jarrón que hemos visto antes?

Vendedor **Ése** valía mil pesetas.

Cliente ¿Y **aquél** otro?

Vendedor Dos mil quinientas. Tienes varios donde elegir.

Cliente No sé.

Actividad 7.17

Here are the complete sentences with the correct answers in bold:

1 Pásame **estas** botas, por favor.

2 Prefiero **este** bañador a **aquél**.

3 ¿Puedo probarme **aquella** chaqueta?

4 ¿Cuánto vale **este** bolso?

5 No me gustan **aquellos** pantalones.

6 **Esta** corbata es más barata que **aquélla.**

7 ¿Me pasa **ese** paquete, por favor?

Actividad 7.18

Here is how you should have matched the words:

gafas–sol: gafas de sol

seda–camisa: camisa de seda / verano / lana

tienda–comestibles: tienda de comestibles

verano–rebajas: rebajas de verano

guantes–piel: guantes de piel / lana / seda

pana–pantalones: pantalones de pana / piel / lana / verano

tarjeta–crédito: tarjeta de crédito

lana–chaqueta: chaqueta de lana / piel / verano / lana / cuero

billetera–cuero: billetera de cuero

Actividad 8.1

Instalaciones y transporte médico	Personal médico	Instrumental	Dolencias	Diagnóstico, remedios y medicamentos
hospital	médico	jeringuilla	dolor de cabeza	venda
ambulancia	enfermera, (- o)	escáner	alergia	operación
sanatorio	doctor	camilla	conmoción	jarabe
Urgencias	pediatra	estetoscopio	herida	pastillas
quirófano	anestesista	bisturí	gripe	análisis
UVI (Unidad de Vigilancia Intensiva)	cirujano	termómetro	catarro	radiografía
	dentista		infección	pomada
			enfermedad	escayola
			constipado	inyección
			fractura	
			apendicitis	

Actividad 8.2

2   The correct sentences are:

(b) Teresa es trasladada al hospital.

(d) Teresa se recupera pronto.

(g) La madre de Teresa se entera del accidente.

(h) La madre de Teresa se siente responsable por lo que ha pasado.

(j) Hay un final feliz.

Actividad 8.3

Here are the correct statements:

1   (c) Omar pide que alguien llame una ambulancia.

2   (b) Teresa recupera el conocimiento al cabo de unas horas.

3   (c) Omar está con Teresa desde el primer momento.

4   (a) Carmen le contó el accidente a doña Amelia.

5   (c) Doña Amelia está arrepentida de su actitud.

6   (c) Teresa y su madre lloran.

Actividad 8.4

Here are the words that match the definitions:

1 ambulancia

2 inconsciente

3 Urgencias

4 fractura

5 descansar

Actividad 8.5

1 These are the phrases about health that Omar and Teresa use:

Omar ¿**Cómo te encuentras**, mi amor?

Teresa […] **Estoy bien**. Siento sólo un pequeño **dolor de cabeza**, pero no es nada.

Omar […] no tienes **nada grave**.

Teresa […] Estoy un poco **conmocionada**, pero no tengo ninguna **fractura**.

2 Here are a few possibilities:

(a) ¿Cómo estás? *(informal)*

¿Cómo está? *(formal)*

¿Qué tal estás? *(informal)*

¿Qué tal está? *(formal)*

¿Cómo te encuentras? *(informal)*

¿Cómo se encuentra? *(formal)*

(b) ¿Te encuentras bien? *(informal)*

¿Se encuentra bien? *(formal)*

(c) ¿Qué te pasa? / ¿Qué te ha pasado? *(informal)*

¿Qué le pasa? / ¿Qué le ha pasado? *(formal)*

(d) ¿Qué te duele? *(informal)*

¿Qué le duele? *(formal)*

(e) ¿Te duele algo? *(informal)*

¿Le duele algo? *(formal)*

Actividad 8.7

1   The facts mentioned about Spanish life are as follows:

   (a) The two films mentioned are *Mujeres al borde de un ataque de nervios* and *¡Ay, Carmela!*

   (b) The actress mentioned is Carmen Maura and the two film directors are Carlos Saura and Pedro Almodóvar.

   (c) The other official languages in Spain apart from Castilian are Basque, Catalan and Galician.

   (d) The painter mentioned is Goya.

   (e) Teresa's mother's shop is *un estanco*.

   (f) One of the big railway stations in Madrid is called Atocha.

2   You may have perceived the tension levels as follows:

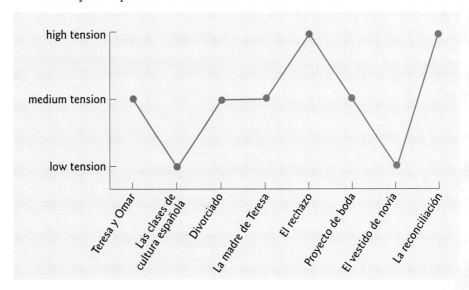

Actividad 8.8

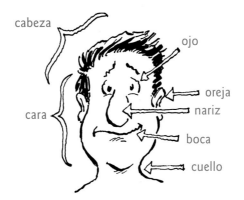

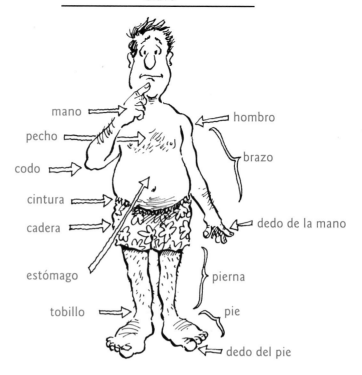

mano — hombro
pecho — brazo
codo
cintura
cadera — dedo de la mano
estómago — pierna
tobillo — pie
— dedo del pie

Actividad 8.9

(a) La aparición de fracturas ante mínimos esfuerzos, como puede ser simplemente estornudar.

(b) Que nuestro organismo está continuamente destruyendo y construyendo pequeñas áreas de tejido óseo.

(c) A partir de los 35–40 años.

(d) Porque este desequilibrio (en la masa ósea) se acentúa de forma exagerada tras la menopausia en las mujeres, ya que los ovarios cesan su actividad hormonal y disminuyen los niveles de estrógenos.

(e) Porque el tratamiento en una fase más avanzada es muy difícil, porque la pérdida de masa ósea es ya demasiado grande.

(f) Con dolor, pérdida de altura y deformidades.

(g) Porque estos signos suelen achacarse muchas veces al proceso natural de envejecimiento.

(h) Actualmente es posible hacer un diagnóstico precoz, gracias al perfeccionamiento de la tecnología existente y al desarrollo de nuevos métodos de diagnóstico.

Actividad 8.10

1   This is how you should have numbered the situations, following the order mentioned on the cassette:

Situation 1: sore throat.

Situation 2: a cold.

Situation 3: bruised finger.

Situation 4: headache.

Situation 5: stomach-ache.

2   Here is the advice you would have given to somebody you knew in each situation:

Situation 1: Tienes que / Debes tomar jarabe. Toma jarabe.

Situation 2: Tienes que acostarte / Debes acostarte y descansar. Acuéstate y descansa.

Situation 3: Tienes que / Debes ir al hospital. Ve al hospital.

Situation 4: Tienes que / Debes tomar una aspirina. Toma una aspirina.

Situation 5: Tienes que / Debes tomar una manzanilla. Toma una manzanilla.

Actividad 8.11

1   You will have noticed that the punctuation (that is, the exclamation marks) was a giveaway. Here is what the different sentences in the imperative convey:

(a) Consejo

(b) Orden

(c) Instrucción

(d) Orden

(e) Consejo

(f) Orden

(g) Consejo

(h) Instrucción

Actividad 8.12

You will have noticed how rhythm has helped you memorize this rhyme. Spanish rhythm is particularly easy to copy because of its regularity.

Actividad 8.13

The table below shows the parts of the body corresponding to the definitions.

1	Son dos órganos internos situados en la parte trasera del cuerpo, cerca de la cintura.	**riñones**
2	Es la parte de abajo de la cara.	**barbilla**
3	Tenemos veinte en el cuerpo.	**uñas**
4	Une la mano al brazo.	**muñeca**
5	Es como un botón en medio del cuerpo.	**ombligo**
6	Los usamos para morder.	**dientes**
7	Sin ella, no podemos hablar.	**lengua**
8	Es un órgano interno, que está a la derecha del estómago.	**hígado**
9	Tenemos dos en la cara, a ambos lados de la nariz.	**mejillas**
10	Los usamos para cerrar los ojos.	**párpados**
11	Es el órgano que bombea la sangre.	**corazón**
12	Tenemos dos, encima de los ojos.	**cejas**
13	Tenemos dos y forman la parte externa de la boca.	**labios**
14	Tenemos muchas, alrededor de los ojos.	**pestañas**
15	El aire que respiramos va a estos órganos.	**pulmones**
16	Es la parte de arriba de la cara.	**frente**

Actividad 8.14

This is what you should have written:

1	Son articulaciones	nudillos, codo
2	Son extremidades	brazos, piernas
3	Están en la mano	pulgar, nudillos, índice
4	Están en la cabeza	dientes, cerebro
5	Está en la parte de atrás	espalda, culo

Actividad 8.15

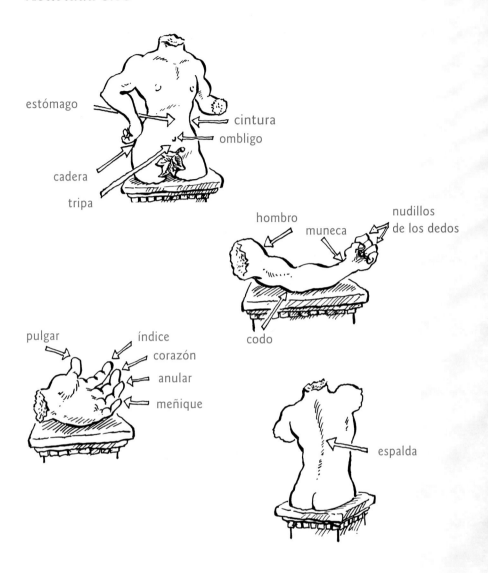

estómago

cintura

ombligo

cadera

tripa

hombro

muneca

nudillos de los dedos

codo

pulgar

índice

corazón

anular

meñique

espalda

Actividad 8.16

This is how you should have matched the parts of the body with their senses and functions:

ojos	la vista	sirven para ver
nariz	el olfato	sirven para oler
oídos	el oído	sirven para oír
boca	el gusto	sirve para saborear
manos	el tacto	sirve para tocar

Actividad 8.17

This is the full text with the correct words in bold:

Hospital de Santa Mercedes

Miércoles, 3 de octubre de 1998

La **paciente** Teresa Martínez ha ingresado esta mañana en el **departamento** de Urgencias. La enferma tenía conmoción y llegó **inconsciente**, pero pasadas unas horas se ha recuperado. Esta tarde se le ha puesto el **termómetro** y tiene un poco de fiebre. Después del examen no se ha encontrado ninguna **fractura**. Tiene un pequeño **corte** en la cabeza, pero no es nada grave. Le he recetado unos sedantes para el **dolor** de cabeza.

Dra. Remedios de Sastre.

Actividad 8.18

1 garganta	ombligo	estómago	pierna
cabeza	hueso	riñones	
2 ambulancia	hospital	camilla	
doctor	enfermera		
3 fractura	dolor	alergia	
4 jarabe	reposo	pastilla	
radiografía	operación		

Acknowledgements

Grateful acknowledgement is made to the following sources for permission to reproduce material in this book:

Text

Page 31: A la lata, al latero, 365 Canciones Infantiles, Copyright © 1991 Grafalco, SA; *page 38*: Canovas, I. H. 1996, *Escuelas de idiomas*, *TECLA*, 24 June 1996, Spanish Embassy Education Department and Birkbeck College, http://www.bbk.ac.uk/Departments/Spanish/TeclaHome.html; *page 97*: Machado, A. 1978, 'La tierra de Alvargonzález', *Poesías completas*, Espasa Calpe, SA; *pages 114–115*: extracted from Roig, A. M. 1995, 'Bocadillos en alza', *El País semanal*, 210, © El País, Quino; *page 119*: extracted from Verdú, V. 1995, 'Familias', *El País semanal*, 2 July 1995, © El País, Verdú, V.; page 150: Baeza, A. 1995, 'Osteoporosis: Una enfermedad en aumento', *Clara*, February 1995, Hymsa, Grupo Editorial Edipresse.

Illustrations

Page 7 (top): Frank Spooner Pictures/Gamma Press; *page 7 (bottom):* Museo Nacional del Prado; *pages 8 (top) and 9 (top):* Kobal Collection; *page 9 (bottom):* Mexicolore; *page 19 (bottom):* Cartoon by Quino, *El País semanal*, 29 December 1996, © Diario El País; *page 26:* Spanish Tourist Office; *page 45:* Ballesta, J. 1996, in *Cambio 16*, 14 October 1996, p. 90, Cambio 16; *page 55:* © Enrique Cerezo PC; page 107: Cartoon by Quino, El País semanal, 29 December 1996, © El País, Quino.

Cartoons by Jim Kavanagh and Ray Webb.

Photos on pages 10, 33, 52, 72, 109, 143 by Roy Lawrance.

Cover photo (of ship) by Max.